THE ONLY ONE

THE ONLY ONE

Said Osman

Editor: Stephen Zimmer

Published by Said Osman

ISBN Number: 9798524698940

Printed in the United States of America

First Edition

Acknowledgements

All praises be to Allah(God) who created everything without anyone's help and who provides every day without people's help.

I would like to thank my dear friend and my brother in faith Nini Mohamed. who connected me to Stephen Zimmer in order to write this book. Writing the book wasn't an easy task. The book took time and research to bring to you something beneficial.

The writer of the book, Said Hassan Osman, put all his effort and time to explain to the reader the deep meaning of Tawhid and its benefits based on the Quran and the saying of the Prophet, peace be upon him. Many friends encouraged me to write this book, for it to be a legacy for the generation to come and a way to spread the goodness of worshipping the creator.

The author of the book took many days to bring a beautiful message to the rest of mankind which is a way for their salvation. After reading this book, you will get a good picture about what the Muslims believe about the oneness of God with evidence from the Holy Quran and the Hadith. Jama was one of the friends who said writing the book is a good idea since the people can learn the message of Islam. The work of this book is a gift to every believer around the corner of the world who believes this unique message about the oneness of Allah.

Introduction

Dear reader, this book will talk about the message of Islam, known as Tawhid (oneness of God).

Tawhid is a unique message about the oneness of God. The religion of Islam is built upon five pillars and Tawhid is one of them. I will take you on a journey with me explaining the deep meaning of Tawhid.

If the person who reads this book works hard on this message, it will be a means of salvation for them . This book will just touch upon some sayings from the Quran and the Hadith to explain what Tawhid really means.

Pre-Islam, people use to worship idols, saints, and images. That is why God sent all messengers to explain this concept to the people, for them to worship God with one heart. This message was very important for the prophets to explain because three hundred and sixty idols were in the Kaaba before Islam came into the Arabian Peninsula.

For this message to take the upper hand, the Muslims had to break the idols in the Kaaba for the people to understand the message without going through idols when praying to Allah[God]. Prophet Muhammad was preaching this message for the rest of his lifetime after he became a messenger through the command of Allah in the cave of Hira.

This Tawhid was taught in different ways, through actions and preaching by the prophet Muhammad during his life when a bedouin called Ghawrath bin Harith took the sword of the Prophet and asked him, "Who will save you from me?" The prophet answered, "Allah," three times. This incident happened when the Prophet came from the Battle of Bani Nadir. The Prophet narrated the history to the companions, telling them to depend on Allah, the one and only,when a calamity came their way.

The oneness of God has different levels which every believer should try to reach in order for the faith to be strong and true. How strong the faith will be is how high the person will be in heaven or in paradise.

Since this book will be about Tawhid, it will talk about the oneness of God in many ways, and it will explain without going to the next step of saying we should follow the prophet Muhammad.

When we talk about Tawhid, the example of Salman al Farsi will come to our mind. Salmantraveled from a far land just to find this beautiful message. Before, he used to worship fire, which his people did for during that time.

Starting from Adam to Noah, people were monotheistic, but after Noah came out to preach people started worshipping their scholars like Wadd Suwa and Yaghuth, as said in the Quran in the verse below.

71:23 Quran

وَقَالُوا لَا تَذَرُنَّ آلِهَتَكُمْ وَلَا تَذَرُنَّ وَدًّا وَلَا سُوَاعًا وَلَا يَغُوثَ وَيَعُوقَ وَنَسْرًا.

"Urging their followers, 'Do not abandon your idols— especialy Wadd, Suwâ', Yaghûth, Ya'ûq, and Nasr.'1.'"Dr.

THE ONLY ONE

Mustafa Khattab, the Clear Quran.

This book will explain this unique message while giving examples and verses to make you understand the concept of Tawhid with the help of God

The Term Tawhid comes from the word Ahad, which means unique one without any partner.

The sources I have in my book will come from the Quran and the sayings of the Prophet. Your job as a reader is to verify their authenticity. The book will include also some examples to make you understand the deep meaning behind Tawhid, so that you will get the full picture of Tawhid.

THE KNOWLEDGE

You have a friend who owns a store. One morning, you go to him and he tells you "I'm going somewhere, look over the store for me until I come back." When a customer comes, you have to tell that customer to wait for the owner because you don't know the price of every item. Just like that, this unique message needs knowledge to understand, that is why God Almighty says in his noble book:

$$ فَاعْلَمْ أَنَّهُ لَا إِلَهَ إِلَّا اللّٰهُ وَاسْتَغْفِرْ لِذَنْبِكَ وَلِلْمُؤْمِنِينَ وَالْمُؤْمِنَاتِ ۗ وَاللَّهُ يَعْلَمُ مُتَقَلَّبَكُمْ وَمَثْوَاكُمْ $$

-Chapter 47 verse 19

So, know well, O Prophet, that there is no god worthy of worship except Allah. And seek forgiveness for your shortcomings1 and for the sins of the believing men and women. For Allah fully knows your movements and places of rest O people." -Dr. Mustafa Khattab, the Clear Quran

Without knowledge of this unique message, the person can't understand the message itself. The scholar Muhammad bin Abdiwahab said in his book called The Three Principles, talking about the three things every one should learn:

الأصول الثلاثة التي يجب على الإنسان معرفتها:

معرفة العبد ربه.

معرفة العبد دينه.

معرفة العبد نبيه.

Every one should know that and learn his God, his religion and his prophet. The knowledge of these three things are connected to each other. Don't be like someone who was left in a store to look over it without knowing the prices of every item, but be smart and learn this unique message from the right sources.

As a car can't be without a manual to understand it, this unique message can't be understood without knowledge. When I say knowledge is very important for this message, I don't mean I'm here to teach but to make you think, as Socrates said, "I cannot teach anybody anything. I can only make them think."

THE ONLY ONE

When I say knowledge is very important for the unique message, that means find the knowledge to know the oneness of the creator.

The greatest companion of prophet Muhammad, Abu Bakr As-Siddiq (RA), , once said, "Knowledge is the life of the mind."

That is why Allah is saying know there is No God but Allah worthy of worship.

"It is not knowledge which should come to you, it is you who should come to the knowledge." Imam Malik

"The highest knowledge is to know that the Almighty is one, without a second one. That is why Allah said in his Holy book,the Quran Had there been other gods besides Allah in the heavens or the earth, both realms would have surely been corrupted. So Glorified is Allah, Lord of the Throne, far above what they claim.(Dr. Mustafa Khattab, the Clear Quran. Chapter 21 verse 22.)

The Way to Salvation

What is salvation to you? Salvation means a lot to many people. This unique message has salvation behind it. If you truly believe it and practice it, you will be saved from hellfire, which is the goal of every believer of this message.

The Almighty Allah says in his book talking about salvation behind this unique message,

"Whoever does evil will be repaid with its like; whoever does good and believes, be it a man or a woman, will enter Paradise and be provided for without measure." 40:40 Quran

"Salvation means to me as a writer to reach the ultimate success and see the creator in the hereafter and to be saved from lhellfire." To quote the Holy Quran. 3:185 Quran

قلى

كل نفس ذائقة الموت وإنما توفون أجوركم يوم القيامة فمن زحزح عن النار وأدخل الجنة فقد فاز وما الحياة الدنيا إلا متاع الغرور

"Every soul shall have a taste of death: And only on the Day of Judgment shall you be paid your full recompense. Only he who is saved far from the Fire and admitted to the Garden will have attained the object (of Life): For the life of this world is but goods and chattels of deception." Yusuf Ali

The prophet Muhammad said, talking about salvation, when he presented this unique message to his uncle Abu Talib in a long saying.

قال أبو بكر : قلت يا رسول الله ، ما نجاة هذا الأمر ؟ فقال رسول الله - صلى الله عليه وسلم - : « من قبل مني الكلمة التي عرضت على عمي فردها ، فهي له نجاة » رواه أحمد .

Abubakar asked, "What is salvation?" The Prophet said, "Anyone who accept from me the word I presented to my uncle and he rejected it. It will be salvation for him."

Salvation comes when we don't associate anything with Godthat can block the salvation we were to get. The wise man Luqman said:

THE ONLY ONE

31:13 Quran

وَإِذْ قَالَ لُقْمَانُ لِابْنِه وَهُوَ يَعِظُهُ يَا بُنَيَّ لَا تُشْرِكْ بِاللَّهِ إِنَّ الشِّرْكَ لَظُلْمٌ عَظِيمٌ

" Luqman counseled his son, 'My son, do not attribute any partners to God: attributing partners to Him is a terrible wrong.' Abdul Haleem

Don't miss getting salvation by associating anything with the creator of the universe and everything in it. The salvation is behind this message and understanding it, so why not work hard for it, to get this salvation.

عَنْ مُعَاذِ بْنِ جَبَلٍ قَالَ : قَالَ رَسُولُ اللَّهِ صَلَّى اللَّهُ عَلَيْهِ وَسَلَّمَ : (مَنْ كَانَ آخِرُ كَلَامِهِ لا إِلَهَ إِلا اللَّهُ دَخَلَ الْجَنَّةَ

Mu'adh bin Jabal narrated that the Prophet said anyone whose last words are there is not worthy of worship except God those who say this definitely will enter paradise.

The Value of This Unique Message

When you want to buy an item you check the value of the item to see if you can buy it or not. We don't want to buy something without value or a good quality. What about the value of a believer of this unique message?

Talking about the value of the believer the Holy Quran said in 4:93 Quran

$$\text{وَمَن يَقْتُلْ مُؤْمِنًا مُّتَعَمِّدًا فَجَزَاؤُهُ جَهَنَّمُ خَالِدًا فِيهَا وَغَضِبَ اللَّهُ عَلَيْهِ وَلَعَنَهُ وَأَعَدَّ لَهُ عَذَابًا عَظِيمًا}$$

"If anyone kills a believer deliberately, the punishment for him is Hell, and there he will remain: God is angry with him, and rejects him, and has prepared a tremendous torment for him". Abdul Haleem

The value of a believer is connected to a punishment, which means no one should harm them, or that person will get five punishments.

13

1. The punishment for him is Hell
2. There he will remain forever
3. God is angry with him
4. God rejects him
5. God has prepared a tremendous torment for him.

This is what the Quran said about the value of a believer. Let us look the other source of Islam, the Hadith.

إِنَّ اللَّهَ حَرَّمَ عَلَيْكُمْ دِمَاءَكُمْ وَأَمْوَالَكُمْ كَحُرْمَةِ يَوْمِكُمْ هَذَا فِي بَلَدِكُمْ هَذَا فِي شَهْرِكُمْ هَذَا" (البخاري

"Allah has made sacred upon you the blood, wealth and honour of each other, just as the sacredness of this day of yours in this land of yours in this month of yours. " (Bukhari)

لزوال الدنيا أهون على الله من قتل رجل مسلم" (رواه الترمذي"

The destruction of the world is lighter on Allah than the killing of one Muslim man", (Tirmidhi)

The honour of a Muslim is very high in the eyes of God, and that is why we shouldn't shed any believer's blood, because he has respect in front of Allah.

To show the value of the believer, he gave some rights that should be kept sacred. For example, if a believer asks you for advice, give him advice.

The Quran is against belitting the value and the honour of a believer of this unique message. Allah gave a command in his book, saying this:

$$\text{يَا أَيُّهَا الَّذِينَ آمَنُوا لَا يَسْخَرْ قَوْمٌ مِّن قَوْمٍ عَسَىٰ أَن يَكُونُوا خَيْرًا مِّنْهُمْ وَلَا نِسَاءٌ مِّن نِّسَاءٍ عَسَىٰ أَن يَكُنَّ خَيْرًا مِّنْهُنَّ}$$

9:11 Quran

"O you who believe, no men should ever scoff at other men. May be, the latter are better than the former. Nor should women (ever scoff) at other women. May be, the latter women are better than the former ones."

Keeping the respect of a believer, Allah commanded not to mock anyone, either male or female, who believes God is one without any associate, because they can be better than the one mocking them.

The teacher of the Quran, the beloved prophet of Allah, said while teaching us and explaining to us the above verse, said in the Hadith:

الْمُسْلِمُ أَخُو الْمُسْلِمِ لاَ يَظْلِمُهُ وَلاَ يَخْذُلُهُ
وَلاَ يَحْقِرُهُ . التَّقْوَى هَا هُنَا » . وَيُشِيرُ إِلَى
صَدْرِهِ ثَلاَثَ مَرَّاتٍ » بِحَسْبِ امْرِئٍ مِنَ
الشَّرِّ أَنْ يَحْقِرَ أَخَاهُ الْمُسْلِمَ كُلُّ الْمُسْلِمِ
عَلَى الْمُسْلِمِ حَرَامٌ دَمُهُ وَمَالُهُ وَعِرْضُهُ »

"A Muslim is the brother of a Muslim. He neither oppresses him, nor humiliates him, nor looks down upon him. The piety is here, (and while saying so he pointed towards his chest thrice). "It is a serious evil for a Muslim that he should look down upon his brother Muslim. All things of a Muslim are inviolable for his brother in faith: his blood, his wealth and his honour."

Before I conclude this chapter. Let us look how the companion of the Prophet practices love and how to value their fellow brothers and sisters in faith.

59:9 Quran

وَالَّذِينَ تَبَوَّءُوا الدَّارَ وَالْإِيمَانَ مِن قَبْلِهِمْ
يُحِبُّونَ مَنْ هَاجَرَ إِلَيْهِمْ وَلَا يَجِدُونَ فِي
صُدُورِهِمْ حَاجَةً مِّمَّا أُوتُوا وَيُؤْثِرُونَ عَلَىٰ
أَنفُسِهِمْ وَلَوْ كَانَ بِهِمْ خَصَاصَةٌ وَمَن

THE ONLY ONE

$$\text{يُوقَ شُحَّ نَفْسِهِ فَأُولَٰئِكَ هُمُ الْمُفْلِحُونَ}$$

"And (the ones) who took their location in the Residence Al-Madînah) and in belief before them, love whomever has migrated to them, (i.e., to the ÉAnsar, the Muslims of Al-Madînah) and do not find in their breasts any need for what has been brought them, (The Muhajirûn, those who emigrated from Makkah) and prefer (the Muhajir?n) above themselves, even though penury be (their portion). And whoever is protected from the avarice of his self, then those are they who are the prosperers."-Dr. Ghali.

This verse was revelead to praise the generosity of the people of Madinah. They used to share everything with the people who came from outside, like the immigrants from Makkah. This verse specifically talks about an event which happens in the time of the Prophet.

A man came to the Prophet and said, "I'm a guest who needs something to eat, so invite me. The Prophet went to all his wives, and they said they don't have anything except water, so the Prophet said, "Who will invite my guest?" A man from the people of Madinah invited him and gave food they prepared for their kids. This example shows how generous they were when a believing brother comes to them, because he has honour in front of Allah.

All Prophets' Message

When God created mankind, he wanted humans to be successful in this world and the one to come. That is why he sent prophets preaching the same message, and that is why their way was one toward God. Let's look some of their words in the Quran about this unique message.

Prophet Noah, or Nuh, talking to his people about the unique message said to his people in 71:3 Quran

أَنِ اعْبُدُوا اللَّهَ وَاتَّقُوهُ وَأَطِيعُونِ.

"Worship Allah alone, fear Him, and obey me. Dr. Mustafa Khattab, the Clear Quran.

The prophets were preaching to worship God alone, fear him and follow all his commandments. That is what Noah told his people for almost one thousand years.

وَلَقَدْ أَرْسَلْنَا نُوحًا إِلَى قَوْمِهِ فَلَبِثَ فِيهِمْ أَلْفَ سَنَةٍ إِلاَّ خَمْسِينَ عَامًا فَأَخَذَهُمُ الطُّوفَانُ وَهُمْ ظَالِمُونَ

19

Indeed, We sent Noah to his people, and he remained among them for a thousand years, less fifty. Then the Flood overtook them, while they persisted in wrongdoing. Dr. Mustafa Khattab, the Clear Quran.

Let's look at another prophet who preached the same message as the rest of the prophets. Abraham, or Ibrahim, the father of faith, preached to Herod and showed him signs that God is one and he should be worshipped.

2:258 Quran

أَلَمْ تَرَ إِلَى الَّذِي حَاجَّ إِبْرَاهِيمَ فِي رَبِّهِ
أَنْ آتَاهُ اللَّهُ الْمُلْكَ إِذْ قَالَ إِبْرَاهِيمُ رَبِّيَ
الَّذِي يُحْيِي وَيُمِيتُ قَالَ أَنَا أُحْيِي وَأُمِيتُ
قَالَ إِبْرَاهِيمُ فَإِنَّ اللَّهَ يَأْتِي بِالشَّمْسِ مِنَ
الْمَشْرِقِ فَأْتِ بِهَا مِنَ الْمَغْرِبِ فَبُهِتَ
الَّذِي كَفَرَ وَاللَّهُ لَا يَهْدِي الْقَوْمَ الظَّالِمِينَ

"Have you not considered the one who argued with Abraham about his Lord [merely] because Allah had given him kingship? When Abraham said, "My Lord is the one who gives life and causes death," he said, "I give life and cause death." Abraham said, "Indeed, Allah brings up the sun from the east, so bring it up from the west." So the disbeliever was overwhelmed [by astonishment], and Allah does not guide the wrongdoing people." - Sahih International

THE ONLY ONE

If we have seen that the message of all the prophets was to worship God alone, without any associate the question is why do people worship something beside the true God. It has to do something with the way some people are raised and how the environment influences them. That is why Allah said in his holy book, in 43:23 Quran

وَكَذَٰلِكَ مَا أَرْسَلْنَا مِن قَبْلِكَ فِي قَرْيَةٍ مِّن نَّذِيرٍ إِلَّا قَالَ مُتْرَفُوهَا إِنَّا وَجَدْنَا آبَاءَنَا عَلَىٰ أُمَّةٍ وَإِنَّا عَلَىٰ آثَارِهِم مُّقْتَدُونَ

"Similarly, whenever We sent a warner to a society before you O Prophet, its spoiled elite would say, "We found our forefathers following a particular way, and we are walking in their footsteps." Dr. Mustafa Khattab, the Clear Quran.

When the unique message comes to us, we should forsake all other ways and believe the evidence which is shown to us. The prophet Said in the Hadith, "Allah's Messenger said, "Both in this world and in the Hereafter, I am the nearest of all the people to Jesus, the son of Mary. The prophets are paternal brothers; their mothers are different, but their religion is one."

عَنْ أَبِي هُرَيْرَةَ، قَالَ قَالَ رَسُولُ اللَّهِ صلى الله عليه وسلم » أَنَا أَوْلَى النَّاسِ بِعِيسَى ابْنِ مَرْيَمَ فِي الدُّنْيَا وَالآخِرَةِ، وَالأَنْبِيَاءُ إِخْوَةٌ لِعَلَّاتٍ، أُمَّهَاتُهُمْ شَتَّى، وَدِينُهُمْ

21

وَاحِدٌ .«

The above Hadith means that all the prophets were preaching the oneness of God starting from Noah to prophet Muhammad, peace be upon all of them. The hadith told us their religion is one, and their preaching was one, but the mothers of them were different.

The Brotherhood

The word "brother" can have many meanings. One meaning is a blood brother, and another one means someone from the same country. This unique message encouraged us to be brothers who should help each other and be united under the faith of the oneness of God. Let's look at what the hadith has to say about this brotherhood in thebelief of the oneness of God.

عن أنس رضي الله عنه عن النبي صلى الله عليه وسلم قال: "لا يؤمن أحدكم حتى يحب لأخيه ما يحب لنفسه» ((متفق عليه)) .

Anas (May Allah be pleased with him) reported:

"The Prophet said, "No one of you becomes a true believer until he likes for his brother what he likes for himself" [Al-Bukhari and Muslim].

To make the society strong and united, the Prophet after he migrated to Madinah, started to build brotherhood between the residents of Madinah and the people who moved from the Makkah, until some of them said take anything you want. The true brotherhood is the brotherhood of believing the oneness of God.

43:67-69 Quran

الْأَخِلَّاءُ يَوْمَئِذٍ بَعْضُهُمْ لِبَعْضٍ عَدُوٌّ إِلَّا الْمُتَّقِينَ

"Close friends will be enemies to one another on that Day, except the righteous," Dr. Mustafa Khattab, the Clear Quran

يا عبادي لا خوف عليكم اليوم ولا أنتم تحزنون

"Who will be told, "O My servants! There is no fear for you Today, nor will you grieve—" Dr. Mustafa Khattab, the Clear Quran

الذين آمنوا بآياتنا وكانوا مسلمين

"Those who believed in Our signs and fully submitted to Us." Dr. Mustafa Khattab, the Clear Quran.

THE ONLY ONE

True brothers are those who fear God and submit their will to God. The true brotherhood is based on the faith of the oneness of God, because what makes the people true brothers according to the above verses are being pious and the belief in One God. The Quran encourages the brotherhood so much, in many places.

وَاعْتَصِمُواْ بِحَبْلِ اللَّهِ جَمِيعًا وَلاَ تَفَرَّقُواْ وَاذْكُرُواْ نِعْمَةَ اللَّهِ عَلَيْكُمْ إِذْ كُنْتُمْ أَعْدَاء فَأَلَّفَ بَيْنَ قُلُوبِكُمْ فَأَصْبَحْتُم بِنِعْمَتِهِ إِخْوَانًا وَكُنْتُمْ عَلَى شَفَا حُفْرَةٍ مِّنَ النَّارِ فَأَنقَذَكُم مِّنْهَا كَذَلِكَ يُبَيِّنُ اللَّهُ لَكُمْ آيَاتِهِ لَعَلَّكُمْ تَهْتَدُونَ

"And hold fast by the covenant of Allah all together and be not disunited, and remember the favor of Allah on you when you were enemies, then He united your hearts so by His favor you became brethren; and you were on the brink of a pit of fire..." [Quran, 3:103]

Islam has always protected and encouraged the sacred act of brotherhood and solidarity – meaning that we must strive for unity and kinship, not only amongst those in the ummah, but also to encourage love and respect for all those around us.

When we take this unique message and practice it, the true brotherhood will come and discrimination will go away, as Bilal bin Rabaha(Ethiopian slave) was given the honor to make the call to prayer when he took the testimony of faith.

25

The true believers of this amazing message, when they understood the message,they put the brotherhood into action. Let us look at an example from the companions.

This event, which I'm going to narrate,happen during the battle of Yarmuk.

The Battle of Yarmuk was a major battle between the army of the Byzantine Empire and the Muslim forces of the Rashidun Caliphate.

During this battle, three men from the Muslim side were about to die, so one of the companions took water to his cousin, but when he found him, someone in need of the water more than the first asked for the water. When they came back to the first man, they found him dead. Their idea of brotherhood was let themselves die and have their brother live, but in this era we changed everything after we misunderstood this beautiful message of there is no god worthy of worship except the one true God.

For the brotherhood to stand, we should forgive our brothers if they did something bad to us. Make supplication for them in order for God to solve to their problems. Asking them to forgive each other and work hard to unite them if there is any problem between them. To tell good and forbid evil is one way to make brotherhood strong and to continue.

$$\text{إِنَّمَا الْمُؤْمِنُونَ إِخْوَةٌ فَأَصْلِحُوا بَيْنَ}$$
$$\text{أَخَوَيْكُمْ وَاتَّقُوا اللَّهَ لَعَلَّكُمْ تُرْحَمُونَ}$$

"The believers are but brothers, so make reconciliation between your brothers and fear Allah that you may receive mercy."
-Surat al-Hujurat 49:10.

وَالْمُؤْمِنُونَ وَالْمُؤْمِنَاتُ بَعْضُهُمْ أَوْلِيَاءُ بَعْضٍ يَأْمُرُونَ بِالْمَعْرُوفِ وَيَنْهَوْنَ عَنِ الْمُنكَرِ وَيُقِيمُونَ الصَّلَاةَ وَيُؤْتُونَ الزَّكَاةَ وَيُطِيعُونَ اللَّهَ وَرَسُولَهُ أُولَٰئِكَ سَيَرْحَمُهُمُ اللَّهُ إِنَّ اللَّهَ عَزِيزٌ حَكِيمٌ .

"The believing men and believing women are allies of one another. They enjoin what is right and forbid what is wrong and establish prayer and give charity and obey Allah and His Messenger. Allah will have mercy upon them, for Allah is Almighty and Wise." -Surat al-Tawba 9:71

يَقُولُونَ رَبَّنَا اغْفِرْ لَنَا وَلِإِخْوَانِنَا الَّذِينَ سَبَقُونَا بِالْإِيمَانِ وَلَا تَجْعَلْ فِي قُلُوبِنَا غِلًّا لِّلَّذِينَ آمَنُوا رَبَّنَا إِنَّكَ رَؤُوفٌ رَّحِيمٌ

"They say: Our Lord, forgive us and our brothers who preceded us in faith and put not in our hearts any resentment toward those who have faith. Our Lord, you are kind and merciful." -Surat al-Hashr 59:10

الْمُسْلِمُونَ كَرَجُلٍ وَاحِدٍ إِنْ اشْتَكَى عَيْنُهُ اشْتَكَى كُلُّهُ وَإِنْ اشْتَكَى رَأْسُهُ اشْتَكَى كُلُّهُ

The Muslims are like a single man. If the eye is afflicted, then the whole body is afflicted. If the head is afflicted, then the whole body is afflicted. Sahih Muslim

The brotherhood can stand when people help each other and solve the problems of their brothers.

$$مَنْ نَفَّسَ عَنْ مُؤْمِنٍ كُرْبَةً مِنْ كُرَبِ الدُّنْيَا نَفَّسَ اللَّهُ عَنْهُ كُرْبَةً مِنْ كُرَبِ يَوْمِ الْقِيَامَةِ وَمَنْ يَسَّرَ عَلَى مُعْسِرٍ يَسَّرَ اللَّهُ عَلَيْهِ فِي الدُّنْيَا وَالْآخِرَةِ وَمَنْ سَتَرَ مُسْلِمًا سَتَرَهُ اللَّهُ فِي الدُّنْيَا وَالْآخِرَةِ وَاللَّهُ فِي عَوْنِ الْعَبْدِ مَا كَانَ الْعَبْدُ فِي عَوْنِ أَخِيهِ$$

"Whoever relieves the hardship of a believer in this world, Allah will relieve his hardship on the Day of Resurrection. Whoever helps ease one in difficulty, Allah will make it easy for him in this world and in the Hereafter. Whoever conceals the faults of a Muslim, Allah will conceal his faults in this world and in the Hereafter. Allah helps the servant as long as he helps his brother." Sahih Muslim

To make supplication for your brothers when they aren't present with you is a form of brotherhood.

Abu Darda reported: The Messenger of Allah, peace and blessings be upon him, said:

$$مَا مِنْ عَبْدٍ مُسْلِمٍ يَدْعُو لِأَخِيهِ بِظَهْرِ$$

THE ONLY ONE

الْغَيْبِ إِلاَّ قَالَ الْمَلَكُ وَلَكَ بِمِثْلٍ

"No Muslim servant supplicates for his brother behind his back but that the angel says: And for you the same." Sahih Muslim

"The true believers when they hear something about their brothers they make excuse for them because they don't know when the people say something about their brothers if it is true or not."

إِذَا بَلَغَكَ عَنْ أَخِيكَ الشَّيْءُ تُنْكِرُهُ
فَالْتَمِسْ لَهُ عُذْرًا وَاحِدًا إِلَى سَبْعِينَ عُذْرًا
فَإِنْ أَصَبْتَهُ وَإِلا قُلْ لَعَلَّ لَهُ عُذْرًا لا أَعْرِفُهُ

"If you hear something from your brother that you reject, make an excuse for him, up to seventy excuses. If you cannot do it, then say: Perhaps he has an excuse I do not know." Shu'ab al-Iman

The brotherhood based on faith has many things behind it which makes the people to talk about the oneness of God Almighty and practice it. Let's look at the example of Noah and his son when they took different ways about believing God and following his commandments.

29

Said Osman

11:45-46 Quran

وَنَادَى نُوحٌ رَّبَّهُ فَقَالَ رَبِّ إِنَّ ابْنِي مِنْ أَهْلِي وَإِنَّ وَعْدَكَ الْحَقُّ وَأَنتَ أَحْكَمُ الْحَاكِمِينَ.

قَالَ يَا نُوحُ إِنَّهُ لَيْسَ مِنْ أَهْلِكَ إِنَّهُ عَمَلٌ غَيْرُ صَالِحٍ فَلَا تَسْأَلْنِ مَا لَيْسَ لَكَ بِهِ عِلْمٌ إِنِّي أَعِظُكَ أَن تَكُونَ مِنَ الْجَاهِلِينَ

"Noah called out to his Lord, saying, "My Lord! Certainly my son is also of my family, Your promise is surely true, and You are the most just of all judges!"

"Allah replied, "O Noah! He is certainly not of your family—he was entirely of unrighteous conduct. So do not ask Me about what you have no knowledge of! I warn you so you do not fall into ignorance." Dr. Mustafa Khattab, the Clear Quran

Father and son took different ways because of faith, so for the brotherhood to continue and to be strong, it should be based on faith all the time. I am not saying we shouldn't respect and welcome other people.

30

THE PROMISE

When you want to tell someone to work hard we use different phrases like "Pull up your socks," which means work hard, or "If you improve, I will get what ever you like." These promises we make for people are for worldly gain, but those who practice the oneness of God and make it the one number priority of their life were given many promises to make them understand the meaning behind their purpose in life. Let's look some of the promises being made for the believers. 6:82 Quran

الَّذِينَ آمَنُواْ وَلَمْ يَلْبِسُواْ إِيمَانَهُم بِظُلْمٍ أُوْلَٰئِكَ لَهُمُ الأَمْنُ وَهُم مُّهْتَدُونَ

"It is only those who are faithful and do not tarnish their faith with falsehood1 who are guaranteed security and are rightly guided." Dr. Mustafa Khattab, the Clear Quran

In this verse, two promises were being made for those who believe God is the only one, without any partner or wife or son, because someone in need needs to have a partner, but God is all powerful. The two promises being made are safety and guidance.

31

Do you want guidance and peace? If your answer is yes, hold unto this unique message. A lot of people flee from their countries because of security and lack of enough food and education, so if we truly practice a good faith without hypocrisy, all the promises will be fulfilled for us with the help of the Almighty God.

7:96 Quran

وَلَوْ أَنَّ أَهْلَ الْقُرَىٰ آمَنُوا وَاتَّقَوْا لَفَتَحْنَا عَلَيْهِم بَرَكَاتٍ مِّنَ السَّمَاءِ وَالْأَرْضِ وَلَٰكِن كَذَّبُوا فَأَخَذْنَاهُم بِمَا كَانُوا يَكْسِبُونَ

"Had the people of those societies been faithful and mindful ☐ of Allah☐, We would have overwhelmed them with blessings from heaven and earth. But they disbelieved, so We seized them for what they used to commit". Dr. Mustafa Khattab, the Clear Quran

The promises of God are true. The question is, are we going to become true believers to get all these promises? Think about it, dear reader.

An amazing promise was being made again in the holy Quran for anyone who believes and does good action, either male or female. Let's see the promise and explain it. 16:97 Quran

مَنْ عَمِلَ صَالِحًا مِّن ذَكَرٍ أَوْ أُنثَىٰ وَهُوَ

THE ONLY ONE

مُؤْمِنٌ فَلَنُحْيِيَنَّهُ حَيَاةً طَيِّبَةً ۖ وَلَنَجْزِيَنَّهُمْ أَجْرَهُم بِأَحْسَنِ مَا كَانُوا يَعْمَلُونَ

"Whoever does good, whether male or female, and is a believer, We will surely bless them with a good life, and We will certainly reward them according to the best of their deeds."- Dr. Mustafa Khattab, the Clear Quran

If you have faith and you did good actions, you will have a good life in this world and the one to come. The belief starts with God is the only one worthy of worship. Good life means to have enough provisions and tranquility and for the people to love you.

قَدْ أَفْلَحَ مَنْ أَسْلَمَ، وَرُزِقَ كَفَافًا، وَقَنَّعَهُ اللهُ بِمَا آتَاه»

"He who submits becomes a Muslim has succeeded, is given sufficient provisions, and is content with Allah for what he is given."

Everyone wants to become successful in this world and to own everything they can, because no one wants to be poor. That is how mankind is. Do you want success? Success comes when you believe God is the only one and you have a good faith. When I say success, I don't mean having everything, but being happy with what you have, which is the oneness of God.

إِنَّ الْإِنسَانَ لَفِي خُسْرٍ

Said Osman

"Man is [deep] in loss," - Abdul Haleem

God's promise for those who believe is that they will not be losers.

$$
إِلاَّ الَّذِينَ آمَنُوا وَعَمِلُوا الصَّالِحَاتِ وَتَوَاصَوْا بِالْحَقِّ وَتَوَاصَوْا بِالصَّبْرِ
$$

"except for those who believe, do good deeds, urge one another to the truth, and urge one another to steadfastness." Abdul Haleem

Those who believe the oneness of Almighty God have another promise which is mentioned in the holy Quran. 4:122 Quran

$$
وَالَّذِينَ ءَامَنُوا وَعَمِلُوا الصَّٰلِحَٰتِ سَنُدْخِلُهُمْ جَنَّٰتٍ تَجْرِى مِن تَحْتِهَا الْأَنْهَٰرُ خَٰلِدِينَ فِيهَآ أَبَدًا وَعْدَ اللَّهِ حَقًّا وَمَنْ أَصْدَقُ مِنَ اللَّهِ قِيلًا
$$

"But the ones who believe and do righteous deeds - We will admit them to gardens beneath which rivers flow, wherein they will abide forever. [It is] the promise of Allah," "[which is] truth, and who is more truthful than Allah in statement." Saheeh International

$$
فَأَمَّا الَّذِينَ ءَامَنُوا وَعَمِلُوا الصَّٰلِحَٰتِ فَيُدْخِلُهُمْ رَبُّهُمْ فِي رَحْمَتِهِۦ ذَٰلِكَ هُوَ الْفَوْزُ الْمُبِينُ ﴿٣٠﴾
$$

The believers have been given a promise, to have the mercy of God.

Allah says, "Then, as for those who believed (in the Oneness of Allah Islamic Monotheism) and did righteous good deeds, their Lord will admit them to His Mercy. That will be the evident success.

When this Nation of Islam practice the tawhid truly they got victory from the Almighty which was promised for them in many places.

40:51 Quran

إِنَّا لَنَنصُرُ رُسُلَنَا وَالَّذِينَ ءَامَنُوا فِي الْحَيَوةِ الدُّنْيَا وَيَوْمَ يَقُومُ الْأَشْهَدُ ﴿٥١﴾

"Indeed, We will support Our messengers and those who believe during the life of this world and on the Day when the witnesses will stand ? - Saheeh International

The promises for the believers are too many for me to mention all of them in this book, so let's conclude with one more before we close this chapter.

وَالَّذِينَ ءَامَنُوا وَعَمِلُوا الصَّلِحَتِ لَنُكَفِّرَنَّ عَنْهُمْ سَيِّـَٔاتِهِمْ وَلَنَجْزِيَنَّهُمْ أَحْسَنَ الَّذِى كَانُوا يَعْمَلُونَ ﴿٧﴾

Their evil will be erased by God, because they believed the oneness of God.

Dear reader, all these promises were made for the people who believe in monotheism. Be one of them, for you to get all these promises.

The Sweetness

A friend invited you to his house and made a good dish for you. When you taste the dish, you will say it is a delicious food because you tasted it. The true message has three things that if you reach them, you will taste the sweetness of faith.

The ones who practice the faith truly will taste this sweetness of the faith. Let us see what these three things are.

عَنْ أَنَسٍ ـ رضى الله عنه ـ عَنِ النَّبِيِّ صلى الله عليه وسلم قَالَ « ثَلَاثٌ مَنْ كُنَّ فِيهِ وَجَدَ حَلَاوَةَ الإِيمَانِ مَنْ كَانَ اللَّهُ وَرَسُولُهُ أَحَبَّ إِلَيْهِ مِمَّا سِوَاهُمَا، وَمَنْ أَحَبَّ عَبْدًا لاَ يُحِبُّهُ إِلاَّ لِلَّهِ، وَمَنْ يَكْرَهُ أَنْ يَعُودَ فِي الْكُفْرِ بَعْدَ إِذْ أَنْقَذَهُ اللَّهُ، كَمَا يَكْرَهُ أَنْ يُلْقَى فِي النَّارِ ».

Said Osman

Narrated by Anas:

The Prophet said, "Whoever possesses the following three qualities will taste the sweetness of faith:

1. The one to whom Allah and His Apostle become dearer than anything else.
2. Who loves a person and he loves him only for Allah's sake.
3. Who hates to revert to disbelief (Atheism) after Allah has brought (saved) him out from it, as he hates to be thrown in fire."

If you want to get the sweetness of faith, love your faith and the messengers more than anyone else. The creator is the one who created you, and that is why we should love him more and obey him in order to get two gifts from him which we need in our life.

3:31 Quran

قُلْ إِن كُنتُمْ تُحِبُّونَ اللَّهَ فَاتَّبِعُونِي يُحْبِبْكُمُ اللَّهُ وَيَغْفِرْ لَكُمْ ذُنُوبَكُمْ وَاللَّهُ غَفُورٌ رَّحِيمٌ.

"Say (O Prophet): "If you really love Allah, then follow me, and Allah shall love you and forgive you your sins. Allah is Most-Forgiving, Very-Merciful." Mufti Taqi Usmani

The second quality to have to get this sweetness of faith is to love a person and love them only for Allah's sake.
Love someone for the sake of the creator, and not for the

sake of race or being from the same tribe, because all these will furnish in this world.

If you love someone because he believes in one creator, then the gift which was promised for both of you is more than you can imagine.

عَنْ أَبِي هُرَيْرَةَ رَضِيَ اللَّهُ عَنْهُ قَالَ: قَالَ رَسُولُ اللَّهِ صَلَّى اللَّهُ عَلَيْهِ وَسَلَّمَ : «إِنَّ اللَّهَ تَبَارَكَ وَتَعَالَى يَقُولُ يَوْمَ الْقِيَامَةِ: أَيْنَ الْمُتَحَابُّونَ بِجَلَالِي؟ الْيَوْمَ أُظِلُّهُمْ فِي ظِلِّي يَوْمَ لَا ظِلَّ إِلَّا ظِلِّي»

رواه البخاري

On the authority of Abu Hurayrah (may Allah be pleased with him), who said that the Messenger of Allah said:

"Allah will say on the Day of Resurrection: Where are those who love one another through My glory? Today I shall give them shade in My shade, it being a day when there is no shade but My shade. It was related by al-Bukhari"

Those who love each other for the sake of the creator will be under the shade of God, when the people need help from God to be saved from hellfire.

The question is, do you love the people for the sake of God or for the material things of this world?

No one wants to be thrown into hellfire, because we cannot

handle it. We should hold onto the oneness of God after he saved us from disbelief, and we should not go back to it.

Ask yourself, do you have these three qualities to taste the sweetness of faith?

After you get the sweetness of faith, there is good news for you from your Lord and fashioner. Let's see what that good news is!

وعن معاذ رضي الله عنه قال: سمعت رسول الله صلى الله عليه وسلم يقول: «قال الله عز وجل: المتحابون في جلالي، لهم منابر من نور يغبطهم النبيون والشهداء».

((رواه الترمذي

Mu'adh (bin Jabal) (May Allah be pleased with him) reported:

Messenger of Allah said, "Allah, the Exalted, has said: 'For those who love one another for the sake of My Glory, there will be seats of light (on the Day of Resurrection), and they will be envied by the Prophets and martyrs." - [At- Tirmidhi]

The oneness of God has different levels which every believer should try to reach in order for the faith to be strong and true. How strong the faith will be is how high the person will be in heaven or paradise.

Imagine getting the honor of sitting on a chair of light

when people are going through hardship because you just love someone for the sake of the creator?

Dear reader for you to taste the sweetness of faith, you should have these three qualities, as follows. Let's ponder upon this saying of the Prophet, peace be upon him.

عَنِ الْعَبَّاسِ بْنِ عَبْدِ الْمُطَّلِبِ، أَنَّهُ سَمِعَ رَسُولَ اللَّهِ صلى الله عليه وسلم يَقُولُ « ذَاقَ طَعْمَ الإِيمَانِ مَنْ رَضِيَ بِاللَّهِ رَبًّا وَبِالإِسْلاَمِ دِينًا وَبِمُحَمَّدٍ نَبِيًّا »

Narrated Al-Abbas bin Abdul-Muttalib: that he heard the Messenger of Allah say: "Whoever is pleased with Allah as (his) Lord, and Islam as (his) religion, and Muhammad as (his) Prophet, then he has tasted the sweetness of faith."

If you are happy with your creator as your lord, and you are pleased with the faith you practice after doing your own research and reading, and the messenger sent to you, then you have tasted the sweetness of faith.

O Believer of God, no one reaches the top without working hard. No one tastes the sweetness of faith until they practice it.

Among the heroes who tasted the flavor of faith was Bilal bin Rabaha, the great companion who was written in the golden books of Islam and the father of steadfastness, may Allah be pleased with him. Let us see what he said about the sweetness of faith

The companions used to ask him this question.

"How were you able to endure such torment without recanting your faith?"

He used to answer their question in this manner and saying.

مَزَجْتُ مَرَارَةَ العَذَابِ بِحَلاوَةِ الإِيمَانِ،
فَطَغَتْ حَلاوَةُ الإِيمَانِ

"The bitterness of torture mixed in me with the sweetness of faith, and the sweetness of faith overcame."

What a beautiful saying, to show us how faith should be high in our life all the time. How to get the sweetness of faith beside the three qualities we mention in this chapter? Let us see some actions. If you do, you can get the sweetness of faith.

Read Quran for meaning

Sometimes people read the Quran just to complete pages. To taste the sweetness of faith read the Quran for meaning. Even though you might read slower this way, it'll be sweet.

To read the Quran while understanding will give you the sweetness of faith. That is why some people, when they read the Quran, cry, because they understand it's meaning.

Build a strong bond with your family.

Call Home

Call your parents or extended family. Express your love. Strengthen your bonds of kinship for the sake of Allah, and you will reap the sweetness.

THE ONLY ONE

47:22 Quran

فَهَلْ عَسَيْتُمْ إِن تَوَلَّيْتُمْ أَن تُفْسِدُوا فِي الأَرْضِ وَتُقَطِّعُوا أَرْحَامَكُمْ.

"So would you perhaps, if you turned away, cause corruption on earth and sever your [ties of] relationship?" -Saheeh international translation

To break the ties with your relatives is forbidden in Islam, and it can lead to not tasting the sweetness of faith.

The first fact about the sweetness of faith is that it is tasted, not seen. To make this fact clear, if you are hungry, and you are presented a very expensive, delicious meal to eat, you will indescribably enjoy every bite of it. The one who watches you will have no idea about the taste of that food, no matter how much he is prudent or wise, will he?

When someone tastes the sweetness of faith, let him not allow anything to distract him or to prevent him from tasting it continuously.

There is a popular saying which goes as follows: "Don't let the shining gold or the painful whips of the whipper distract you from your goal."

How do you know if you tasted the sweetness of faith? This question is for you to think about, dear reader.

When the believers of the oneness of God taste the sweetness of faith, their conditions will change of how they think about faith.

The Prophet asked Harith bin Malik how is his morning? Harith replied. "I'm a true believer this morning." The Prophet said every claim has reality (proof), what is the proof for your claim?

He replied with an amazing answer, which shows he tasted the sweetness of faith.

"Since this morning, I have distanced myself from the world, I spent my night awake in worship and my day fasting. Such is my conviction, that I can almost see the throne of my lord being brought to accountability, the day of judgment. Such is my conviction that I can almost see the inhabitants of paradise visiting one another therein, and I can hear the inhabitants of hellfire screaming. The prophet said to him, "You are a slave whose heart has been illuminated with belief. Remain steadfast on this perception of yours."

The True Believers

When we hear the term belief, we question about faith and the things surrounding it. In this chapter, we will learn with the help of God the qualities of those who truly believe the oneness of God, because the book is all about this unique message.

There are true believers, and there are false believers who claim a faith but don't practice it. The criteria to know the true believers was mentioned in several verses from the holy Quran. Let's ponder them and think deeply.

إِنَّمَا الْمُؤْمِنُونَ الَّذِينَ آمَنُوا بِاللَّهِ وَرَسُولِهِ ثُمَّ لَمْ يَرْتَابُوا وَجَاهَدُوا بِأَمْوَالِهِمْ وَأَنفُسِهِمْ فِي سَبِيلِ اللَّهِ ۚ أُولَٰئِكَ هُمُ الصَّادِقُونَ

"The believers are only those who have believed in Allah and His Messenger and then doubt not but strive with their properties and their lives in the cause of Allah It is those who are the truthful" -[al-Hujurat (49): 15]

The true believers believe God Almighty and the messenger sent to them without any doubt, and they give to the needy when they can, because it is a sign of the true faith they have for God. The true believers don't have any doubts because they search and learn more about the oneness of God and the things around them which show the power of the creator.

Let's look some of the amazing qualities of the true believers mentioned in the eighth chapter of the Quran called Al-anfal.

8:2 Quran

إِنَّمَا الْمُؤْمِنُونَ الَّذِينَ إِذَا ذُكِرَ اللَّهُ وَجِلَتْ قُلُوبُهُمْ وَإِذَا تُلِيَتْ عَلَيْهِمْ آيَاتُهُ زَادَتْهُمْ إِيمَانًا وَعَلَى رَبِّهِمْ يَتَوَكَّلُونَ.

The true believers are only those whose hearts tremble at the remembrance of Allah, whose faith increases when His revelations are recited to them, and who put their trust in their Lord. Dr. Mustafa Khattab, the Clear Quran

In this verse, three qualities are mentioned. Just ask yourself, do you have one of them, to say that you believe in this unique message which will connect you to your creator?

The oneness of God and prayer go hand in hand. That Is why God says in the next verse that they establish prayer, which means they pray correctly as shown by the Prophet and they give what they have.

8:3 Quran

الَّذِينَ يُقِيمُونَ الصَّلاةَ وَمِمَّا رَزَقْنَاهُمْ يُنفِقُونَ.

They are those who establish prayer and donate from what We have provided for them." Dr. Mustafa Khattab, the Clear Quran

The subject of this chapter is about who is a true believer. God is giving the answer and makes a promise for them. Let's ponder on this wonderful verse. 8:4 Quran

أُوْلَئِكَ هُمُ الْمُؤْمِنُونَ حَقًّا لَّهُمْ دَرَجَاتٌ عِندَ رَبِّهِمْ وَمَغْفِرَةٌ وَرِزْقٌ كَرِيمٌ.

"It is they who are the true believers. They will have elevated ranks, forgiveness, and an honourable provision from their Lord." Dr. Mustafa Khattab, the Clear Quran

The true believers will get their ranks elevated in paradise, and they will get forgiveness of sins and provisions from God Almighty because of the truthfulness of their faith.

Still, we are talking about what are the signs of the true believers who believe the oneness of God.

THE ONLY ONE

9:71 Quran

وَالْمُؤْمِنُونَ وَالْمُؤْمِنَاتُ بَعْضُهُمْ أَوْلِيَاءُ
بَعْضٍ يَأْمُرُونَ بِالْمَعْرُوفِ وَيَنْهَوْنَ عَنِ
الْمُنْكَرِ وَيُقِيمُونَ الصَّلَاةَ وَيُؤْتُونَ الزَّكَاةَ
وَيُطِيعُونَ اللَّهَ وَرَسُولَهُ أُولَئِكَ سَيَرْحَمُهُمُ
اللَّهُ إِنَّ اللَّهَ عَزِيزٌ حَكِيمٌ.

"The believers, both men and women, are guardians of one another. They encourage good and forbid evil, establish prayer and pay alms-tax, and obey Allah and His Messenger. It is they who will be shown Allah's mercy. Surely Allah is Almighty, All-Wise." Dr. Mustafa Khattab, the Clear Quran

The true believers are helpers of each other and they command good, forbid evil, establish prayer, and they give charity while obeying Allah and his messenger. Those will have mercy from God.

The true believers were given a lot of qualities, which they received after they believed truly the oneness of God. Let's see this amazing verse from chapter forty-nine called "hujurat," meaning rooms.

49:15 Quran

إِنَّمَا الْمُؤْمِنُونَ الَّذِينَ آمَنُوا بِاللَّهِ وَرَسُولِهِ ثُمَّ لَمْ يَرْتَابُوا وَجَاهَدُوا بِأَمْوَالِهِمْ وَأَنفُسِهِمْ فِي سَبِيلِ اللَّهِ أُوْلَئِكَ هُمُ الصَّادِقُونَ.

"The true believers are the ones who have faith in God and His Messenger and leave all doubt behind, the ones who have struggled with their possessions and their persons in God's way: they are the ones who are true."

They are the truthful believers, because they believe God is one, without a second association, and that is why someone who doesn't believe in God has a lot of doubts. The book Psalms said in chapter 14 verse 1:

'Only fools say in their hearts, "There is no God." They are corrupt, and their actions are evil; not one of them does good."
-New Living Translation

The true believers are wise and not fools, and that is why they were given a lot of promises and qualities in the holy Quran. After reading the verses, think about your faith. Do you truly believe the oneness of God? Or do you mix with something which isn't pure, like worshipping idols?

The golden question is, how to become a true believer?

Believe in the unseen:

The first characteristic of a believer is to believe in Allah — The One True God who created everything. It is this belief that propels other articles of faith which cannot be seen. This includes the belief in Angels, prophets, revelations, resurrection and destiny — either good or bad. And this is why God puts it clear thus:

What makes someone a true believer is if they believe the unseen, which is called "Ghaib" in Islam.

To show humility is one way to become a true believer.

The believers are humble and kind in character. They exhibit the most beautiful traits in human personality. The best example can be seen from the life of Muhammad (peace be upon him). Many people came to accept Islam from his excellent traits. He once said:"He is not one of us, the one who is not merciful to the young and respectful to the elderly" (Tirmidhi).

Since we have seen true believers of the oneness of God, what makes someone not to be a true believer?

2:8 Quran

وَمِنَ النَّاسِ مَن يَقُولُ آمَنَّا بِاللَّهِ وَبِالْيَوْمِ الْآخِرِ وَمَا هُم بِمُؤْمِنِينَ

"And there are some who say, "We believe in Allah and the Last Day," yet they are not true believers." Dr. Mustafa Khattab, the Clear Quran

Some people claim they are true believers, but they aren't,

49

because of not practicing the faith and committing deception of the believers.

2:9 Quran

يُخَادِعُونَ اللَّهَ وَالَّذِينَ آمَنُوا وَمَا يَخْدَعُونَ إِلَّا أَنفُسَهُمْ وَمَا يَشْعُرُونَ

"They seek to deceive Allah and the believers, yet they only deceive themselves, but they fail to perceive it." Dr. Mustafa Khattab, the Clear Quran

They claim they are believers so that they can deceive God and the believers, but they have sickness in their heart of hypocrisy and lying. That is what shows they are not true believers.

2:10 Quran

فِي قُلُوبِهِم مَّرَضٌ فَزَادَهُمُ اللَّهُ مَرَضًا وَلَهُمْ عَذَابٌ أَلِيمٌ بِمَا كَانُوا يَكْذِبُونَ

There is sickness in their hearts, and Allah only lets their sickness increase. They will suffer a painful punishment for their lies. Dr. Mustafa Khattab, the Clear Quran

Their heart has sickness in it, and that is why they are not true believers. They disbelieve the verses of Almighty God and his oneness.

They are not true believers Because when the truth of God is presented to them, instead of belief, they insult the believers who believe Oneness of God.

2:13 Quran

"And when they are told, "Believe as others believe," they reply, "Will we believe as the fools believe?" Indeed, it is they who are fools, but they do not know." Dr. Mustafa Khattab, the Clear Quran.

They are not true believers because they are double-faced people who don't want to believe but act like they are believers.

2:14 Quran

وَإِذَا لَقُواْ الَّذِينَ آمَنُواْ قَالُواْ آمَنَّا وَإِذَا خَلَوْا إِلَى شَيَاطِينِهِمْ قَالُواْ إِنَّا مَعَكُمْ إِنَّمَا نَحْنُ مُسْتَهْزِؤُونَ.

"When they meet the believers they say, "We believe." But when alone with their evil associates they say, "We are definitely with you; we were only mocking." Dr. Mustafa Khattab, the Clear Quran

They aren't true believers because they trade guidance for

51

misguidance, and while they trade guidance for misguidance, they will not benefit from anything.

Let's conclude this chapter with this example, to show how people who act like they believe but don't believe what God said about them.

2:17 Quran

مَثَلُهُمْ كَمَثَلِ الَّذِي اسْتَوْقَدَ نَارًا فَلَمَّا أَضَاءَتْ مَا حَوْلَهُ ذَهَبَ اللَّهُ بِنُورِهِمْ وَتَرَكَهُمْ فِي ظُلُمَاتٍ لاَّ يُبْصِرُونَ.

"Their example is that of someone who kindles a fire, but when it lights up all around them, Allah takes away their light, leaving them in complete darkness—unable to see." Dr. Mustafa Khattab, the Clear Quran.

When the truth comes, God leaves them in darkness because of their disbelief, and they will be unable to see the truth because they are willfully deaf and dumb.

THE RIGHTS

We hear all the time about knowing your rights as a citizen or someone who is a resident of a country. The rights of this unique message to know them is very important.

The Prophet asked Mu'adh bin Jabal once, "Do you know the rights of Allah upon the creation and the rights of the creation upon Allah?" Muad said Allah and his messenger know best.

وعن معاذ بن جبل ، رضي الله عنه ، قال: كنت ردف النبي صلى الله عليه وسلم، على حمار فقال: « يا معاذ هل تدري ما حق الله على عباده، وما حق العباد على الله. ؟ قلت: الله ورسوله أعلم. قال:»فإن حق الله على العباد

أن يعبدوه، ولا يشركوا به شيئاً، وحق العباد على الله أن لا يعذب من لا يشرك به شيئاً، فقلت، يا رسول الله أفلا أبشر الناس؟ قال لا تبشرهم فيتكلوا» ((متفق عليه)) .

Mu'adh bin Jabal (May Allah be pleased with him) reported: "I was riding a pillion with the Prophet on a donkey. He said, "O Mu'adh, do you know what is the right of Allah upon His slaves, and what is the Right of His slaves upon Allah?" I said: "Allah and His Messenger know better". Upon this the Messenger of Allah said, "Allah's Right upon His slaves is that they should worship Him Alone and associate nothing with Him; and His slaves' right upon Him is that He should not punish who does not associate a thing with Him." He (Mu'adh) added: I said to the Messenger of Allah: "Shall I give the glad tidings to people?" He said, "Do not tell them this good news for they will depend on it alone".

The rights of Allah upon the creation is to worship Him without any association. The rights of mankind upon God is to put in paradise anyone who doesn't associate anything with him.

The Prophet said, talking about this unique message of oneness of God:

عَنْ عُثْمَانَ قَالَ قَالَ رَسُولُ اللَّه صَلَّى اللَّهُ عَلَيْهِ وَسَلَّمَ (مَنْ مَاتَ وَهُوَ يَعْلَمُ أَنْ لَا إِلَهَ إِلا اللَّهُ دَخَلَ الْجَنَّةَ)

Anyone who dies while knowing there is none worthy of worship except God enters paradise (related by Muslim). This message has salvation behind it, so it is very important to learn the rights of the message.

Worshipping idols, images, and saints is going against the rights of this message and giving the worship to someone else beside the creator.

If someone breaks these rights he can destroy all his actions.

39:65 Quran

وَلَقَدْ أُوحِيَ إِلَيْكَ وَإِلَى الَّذِينَ مِنْ قَبْلِكَ لَئِنْ أَشْرَكْتَ لَيَحْبَطَنَّ عَمَلُكَ وَلَتَكُونَنَّ مِنَ الْخَاسِرِينَ

"It has already been revealed to you—and to those prophets before you—that if you associate others with Allah, your deeds will certainly be void and you will truly be one of the losers."

The rights of the message are having complete knowledge about it and not associating anything with your creator, because it will destroy all actions. You have to accept every command of this message, starting with establishing the prayer.

Believers should love the message more than anything else, and they should talk about it to know its rights and what nullifies it. Believers should stay away from the hypocrisy of showing belief but having something different in their heart.

Anyone who doesn't understand the rights of the message that there is no one who has the right to be worshipped except the only true God, that person's abode will not be with God Thatis why they will be confused on the day of judgment, rejecting what they used to worship.

21:22 Quran

لَوْ كَانَ فِيهِمَا آلِهَةٌ إِلَّا اللَّهُ لَفَسَدَتَا فَسُبْحَانَ اللَّهِ رَبِّ الْعَرْشِ عَمَّا يَصِفُونَ

"Had there been other gods besides Allah in the heavens or the earth, both realms would have surely been corrupted. So Glorified is Allah, Lord of the Throne, far above what they claim." Dr. Mustafa Khattab, the Clear Quran

The right is not to take my worship to anyone, so don't give it to anyone other than Allah. Taking the worship to someone else is a great mistake, according to the holy Quran.

وَإِذْ قَالَ لُقْمَانُ لِابْنِهِ وَهُوَ يَعِظُهُ يَا بُنَيَّ لَا تُشْرِكْ بِاللَّهِ إِنَّ الشِّرْكَ لَظُلْمٌ عَظِيمٌ

31:13 Quran

"And remember when luqman said to his son, while advising him, "O my dear son! Never associate anything with Allah in worship, for associating others with Him is truly the worst of all wrongs." Dr. Mustafa Khattab, the Clear Quran

KNOW HIM WELL

When you spend time with someone, at least you will know their likes and dislikes. Allah in the Quran teaches us his oneness in many places, which is know him well and worship him because he is the one who created you all for his worship.

51:56 Quran

وَمَا خَلَقْتُ الْجِنَّ وَالْإِنسَ إِلَّا لِيَعْبُدُونِ

"I did not create jinn and humans except to worship Me." Dr. Mustafa Khattab, the Clear Quran

To know him well is to talk about him every time, because as much as we talk about him, his love and following his commandments will be seen in our life. it will be easy for us to obey him, and that is why we see many examples written in the Holy Quran talk about the oneness of God and knowing him more.

2:163 Quran

وَإِلَٰهُكُمْ إِلَٰهٌ وَاحِدٌ ۖ لَّا إِلَٰهَ إِلَّا هُوَ الرَّحْمَٰنُ الرَّحِيمُ

Sahih International: "And your god is one God. There is no deity [worthy of worship] except Him, the Entirely Merciful, the Especially Merciful."

The great scholar ibn Kathir explains this verse as follows:.

"In this Ayah, Allah mentions that He is the only deity, and that He has no partners or equals. He is Allah, the One and Only, the Sustainer, and there is no deity worthy of worship except Him. He is the Most Gracious Ar-Rahman, the Most Merciful ☐ Ar-Rahim."

For us to know him well, he put some proofs for his oneness and existence and that is why he is saying:

41:53 Quran

سَنُرِيهِمْ آيَاتِنَا فِي الْآفَاقِ وَفِي أَنفُسِهِمْ حَتَّىٰ يَتَبَيَّنَ لَهُمْ أَنَّهُ الْحَقُّ ۗ أَوَلَمْ يَكْفِ بِرَبِّكَ أَنَّهُ عَلَىٰ كُلِّ شَيْءٍ شَهِيدٌ

THE ONLY ONE

"We will show them Our signs in the horizons and within themselves until it becomes clear to them that it is the truth. But is it not sufficient concerning your Lord that He is, over all things, a Witness?

To know him well he made it easy for us and put evidence in the horizons and within ourselves until everything about the Quran which talks about his oneness is clear to us."

How to know our creator is the question we should ask ourselves.

There are many ways to know our creator and talking about his greatness is one of them, including looking around us to see how beautiful his creation is. That is why when we understand the beauty of the creation, we can realize the one behind everything and his oneness.

To know him well, a lot of people talk about his greatness, and one of them is the great scholar Ibn al-Qayyim. Let me quote it here

"He is controlling the affairs of all the kingdoms. He commands and prohibits, creates and gives provision, and gives death and gives life. He raises and lowers people's status, alternates night and day, gives days (good and not so good) to men by turns, and causes nations to rise and fall, so that one nation vanishes and another emerges. His command and decree are carried out throughout the heavens and on earth, above it and below it, in the oceans and in the air. He has knowledge of all things and knows the number of all things. He hears all voices, and does not mistake one for another; He hears them all, in all the different languages and with all their varied requests and pleas. No voice distracts Him from hearing another, He does not confuse their requests, and He never tires of hearing the pleas of those in need. He sees all that is visible, even the walk of a black ant across a solid rock in the darkest night.

To sit in the gathering where people talk about God and his oneness is another way to learn more about him because we will gain knowledge of our creator."

18:28 Quran

وَاصْبِرْ نَفْسَكَ مَعَ الَّذِينَ يَدْعُونَ رَبَّهُم بِالْغَدَاةِ وَالْعَشِيِّ يُرِيدُونَ وَجْهَهُ وَلَا تَعْدُ عَيْنَاكَ عَنْهُمْ تُرِيدُ زِينَةَ الْحَيَاةِ الدُّنْيَا وَلَا تُطِعْ مَنْ أَغْفَلْنَا قَلْبَهُ عَن ذِكْرِنَا وَاتَّبَعَ هَوَاهُ وَكَانَ أَمْرُهُ فُرُطًا.

"And keep yourself patient [by being] with those who call upon their Lord in the morning and the evening, seeking His countenance. And let not your eyes pass beyond them, desiring adornments of the worldly life, and do not obey one whose heart We have made heedless of Our remembrance and who follows his desire and whose affair is ever [in] neglect."

"And keep yourself patiently with those who call on their Lord morning and afternoon, seeking His Face;) meaning, sit with those who remember Allah, who say "La Ilaha Illallah," who praise Him, glorify Him, declare His greatness and call on Him, morning and evening, all the servants of Allah, whether rich or poor, strong or weak. It was said that this was revealed about the nobles of Quraysh when they asked the Prophet to sit with them on his own, and not to bring his weak Companions with him, such as Bilal, Ammar Suhayb, Khabbab and Ibn Mas'ud. They wanted him to sit with them on his own, but Allah forbade him from doing that.

When we sit in a gathering where people talk about the oneness it is a way to boost our faith and praise him. That is why

God says he will forgive these who sit in these gatherings.

Anas bin Malik says, narrating from the Prophet, peace be upon him, that he said in a hadith

ما من قوم اجتمعوا يذكرون الله عز وجل لا يريدون بذلك إلا وجهه إلا ناداهم مناد من السماء أن قوموا مغفورا لكم قد بدلت سيئاتكم حسنات.

"There is not a people who gather somewhere remembering God just to please him a Caller will call from the heaven saying stand up all your sins have been changed to good ones."

To know him more is about having good friends who make you remember him and his oneness while you are sitting with them, because they make sure you are closer to him, whenever you meet them.

Talking about the oneness of God, standing, sitting and lying on their side means talking about the oneness of God everywhere, not in just one place or in one way. To look around and praise God for his beautiful creation is one way to talk about his oneness, as we can see from the verse below.

3:191 Quran

الَّذِينَ يَذْكُرُونَ اللَّهَ قِيَامًا وَقُعُودًا وَعَلَىٰ

جُنُوبِهِمْ وَيَتَفَكَّرُونَ فِي خَلْقِ السَّمَاوَاتِ وَالْأَرْضِ رَبَّنَا مَا خَلَقْتَ هَٰذَا بَاطِلًا سُبْحَانَكَ فَقِنَا عَذَابَ النَّارِ

"Who remember Allah while standing or sitting or [lying] on their sides and give thought to the creation of the heavens and the earth, [saying], "Our Lord, You did not create this aimlessly; exalted are You [above such a thing]; then protect us from the punishment of the Fire.— Saheeh International

When we talk about the oneness of God, we mean in Tawhid that he doesn't have son nor holy spirit nor is he a father. That is the pure oneness of God we will talk in this book.

This oneness means nothing looks like him, because he is above everything and he is creator of everything, without copying from anyone, or getting help from anybody.

بسم الله الرحمن الرحيم

قُلْ هُوَ اللَّهُ أَحَدٌ

اللَّهُ الصَّمَدُ

لَمْ يَلِدْ وَلَمْ يُولَدْ

THE ONLY ONE

وَلَمْ يَكُن لَّهُ كُفُوًا أَحَدٌ

Say: "He is Allah, [who is] One.
Allah, the Eternal Refuge.
He neither begets nor is born,
Nor is there to Him any equivalent."

For us to get a good picture of this concept of Tawhid, we have to ponder upon this chapter called ikhlas, meaning "The Sincerity," which was revealed when the non-believers asked "What does your God look like, who you want us to worship? Is he made of gold or stick or other materials?" The answer given was that he is one without a second, and he isn't like anything which comes to our mind that is why he says in 42:11 Quran

فَاطِرُ السَّمَاوَاتِ وَالْأَرْضِ ۚ جَعَلَ لَكُم مِّنْ أَنفُسِكُمْ أَزْوَاجًا وَمِنَ الْأَنْعَامِ أَزْوَاجًا يَذْرَؤُكُمْ فِيهِ ۚ لَيْسَ كَمِثْلِهِ شَيْءٌ ۖ وَهُوَ السَّمِيعُ الْبَصِيرُ

"He is] Creator of the heavens and the earth. He has made for you from yourselves, mates, and among the cattle, mates; He multiplies you thereby. There is nothing like unto Him,1 and He is the Hearing, the Seeing."2

THE BRANCHES OF FAITH

When you look at a tree growing, you will see different parts of the tree, like branches and roots. Just like a tree, the faith has different levels to it which go up to seventy branches or more.

عَنْ أَبِي هُرَيْرَةَ، قَالَ قَالَ رَسُولُ اللَّهِ صلى الله عليه وسلم « الإِيمَانُ بِضْعٌ وَسَبْعُونَ شُعْبَةً فَأَفْضَلُهَا لاَ إِلَهَ إِلاَّ اللَّهُ وَأَدْناها إِمَاطَةُ الأَذَى عَنِ الطَّرِيقِ وَالْحَيَاءُ شُعْبَةٌ مِنَ الإِيمَانِ » .

The Messenger of Allāh said:

"There are over 70 branches of faith. The highest is to bear witness that 'There is no god but Allāh and Muhammad is the Messenger of Allāh' (lā ilāha illallāhu Muhammadur rasūlullāh). The lowest is the removal of harm from the road. Modesty is also of faith."

The faith, as we can see, has branches according to the

hadith, and the highest one is to bear witness. No one has the right to be worshipped except the one, only true God, because it is the key to every goodness. The belief of the oneness of God should include following the messengers when God sends them to the people.

The lowest one is to protect the society from harm by picking up the unwanted things on the street like broken bottles and other things which can harm. Not doing things which displease God is part of Faith.

Since the oneness of God is the key is to every success we make in this world and hereafter, we should try to keep this success without losing it, in order to open the gates of paradise with it.

Let's come back to the saying of the prophets about the branches of faith and see what these branches are while naming them. So, dear reader, I ask your forgiveness, if it is a long list to read. Here we go, let's name them one by one with the help of Allah.

While talking about the branches of faith, we will include some proof to some of them to help you understand.

To believe in Allāh Most High.

2:136 Quran

قُولُوا آمَنَّا بِاللَّهِ

Say (O, Muslims): "We believe in Allah

To believe that everything other than Allāh was nonexistent. Thereafter, Allāh Most High created these things, and subsequently they came into existence.

To believe in the existence of angels.

To believe that all the heavenly books that were sent to the different prophets are true. However, apart from the Qur'an, all other books are not valid anymore.

To believe that all the prophets are true. However, we are commanded to follow the Prophet Muhammad alone.

To believe that Allāh Most High has knowledge of everything from beforehand and that only that which He sanctions or wishes will occur.

To believe that Resurrection will definitely occur.

To believe in the existence of Paradise.

To believe in the existence of Hell.

To have love for Allāh Most High.

Said Osman

To have love for the Messenger of Allāh.

To love or hate someone solely because of Allāh.

To execute all actions with the intention of religion alone.

To regret and express remorse when a sin is committed.

To fear Allāh Most High.

To hope for the mercy of Allāh Most High

To be modest.

To express gratitude over a bounty or favour.

To fulfill promises.

To exercise patience.

THE ONLY ONE

To consider yourself lower than others.

To have mercy on the creation.

To be pleased with whatever you experience from Allāh Most High.

To place your trust in Allāh Most High.

Not to boast or brag over any quality that you posses.

Not to have malice or hatred towards anybody.

Not to be envious of anyone.

Not to become angry.

Not to wish harm for anyone.

Not to have love for the world.

Said Osman

To recite the Testimony of Faith [*Kalimatu- Shahādah*] with the tongue.

To recite the Qur'ān.

To acquire knowledge.

To pass on knowledge.

To make supplications [du'a] to Allāh Most High.

To make invocations [dhikr] of Allāh Most High.

To abstain from the following:

> Lies
> Backbiting
> Vulgar words,
> Cursing
> Singing that is contrary to the Sharī'ah

To make ablution [wudū], take bath [ghusl], and keep one's clothing clean.

THE ONLY ONE

To be steadfast in offering the prayer [salāt].

To pay the tithe [zakāt] and Sadaqatu-l Fitr.

To fast.

To perform the Hajj

To make i'tikāf.

To move away or migrate from that place which is harmful for one's religion [deen]

To fulfill the vows that have been made to Allāh Most High.

To fulfill the oaths that are not sinful.

To pay the expiation [kaffārah] for unfulfilled oaths.

To cover those parts of the body that are obligatory [*fard*] to cover.

Said Osman

To perform the ritual slaughter [Udhiya/Qurbani].

To enshroud and bury the deceased.

To pay back your debts.

To abstain from prohibited things when undertaking monetary transactions.

To NOT conceal something true which you may have witnessed.

To get married when the *nafs* desires to do so.

To fulfill the rights of those who are under you.

To provide comfort to one's parents.

To rear children in the proper manner

To NOT sever relations with one's friends and relatives.

To obey one's master.

To be just.

To NOT initiate any way that is contrary to that of the generality of the Muslims.

To obey the ruler, provided what he orders is not contrary to the *Shari'ah*.

To make peace between two warring groups or individuals.

49:9 Quran

وَإِن طَائِفَتَانِ مِنَ الْمُؤْمِنِينَ اقْتَتَلُوا فَأَصْلِحُوا بَيْنَهُمَا فَإِن بَغَتْ إِحْدَاهُمَا عَلَى الْأُخْرَى فَقَاتِلُوا الَّتِي تَبْغِي حَتَّى تَفِيءَ إِلَى أَمْرِ اللَّهِ فَإِن فَاءَتْ فَأَصْلِحُوا بَيْنَهُمَا بِالْعَدْلِ وَأَقْسِطُوا إِنَّ اللَّهَ يُحِبُّ

Said Osman

الْمُقْسِطِينَ.

"And if two parties of believers fall to fighting, then make
peace between them. And if one party of them doeth wrong
to the other, fight ye that which doeth wrong till it return unto
the ordinance of Allah; then, if it return, make peace between
them justly, and act equitably. Lo! Allah loveth the equitable."

To assist in noble tasks

To command the good and forbid the evil.

3:104 Quran

وَلْتَكُن مِّنكُمْ أُمَّةٌ يَدْعُونَ إِلَى الْخَيْرِ
وَيَأْمُرُونَ بِالْمَعْرُوفِ وَيَنْهَوْنَ عَنِ الْمُنكَرِ
وَأُولَٰئِكَ هُمُ الْمُفْلِحُونَ

"Let there arise out of you a band of people inviting to all that
is good, enjoining what is right, and forbidding what is wrong:
They are the ones to attain felicity." -Yusuf Ali

To mete out punishments according to the Shari'ah, IF it is

the government.

2:190 Quran.

وَقَاتِلُواْ فِي سَبِيلِ اللَّهِ الَّذِينَ يُقَاتِلُونَكُمْ وَلاَ تَعْتَدُواْ إِنَّ اللَّهَ لاَ يُحِبُّ الْمُعْتَدِينَ.

Fight in the way of Allah those who fight you but do not transgress. Indeed. Allah does not like transgressors.

To fight the enemies of religion [*deen*] whenever such an occasion presents itself.

To fulfill one's trusts (amana).

2:40 Quran.

يَا بَنِي إِسْرَائِيلَ اذْكُرُواْ نِعْمَتِيَ الَّتِي

أَنْعَمْتُ عَلَيْكُمْ وَأَوْفُواْ بِعَهْدِي أُوفِ

بِعَهْدِكُمْ وَإِيَّايَ فَارْهَبُونِ.

"O Children of Israel! Remember My favour wherewith I favoured you, and fulfil your (part of the) covenant, I shall fulfil My (part of the) covenant, and fear Me." - Pickthall

To give loans to those who are in need.

To see to the needs of one's neighbour.

To ensure that one's income is pure.

To spend according to the Sharī'ah.

4:86 Quran

To reply to one who has greeted you.

وَإِذَا حُيِّيتُم بِتَحِيَّةٍ فَحَيُّوا بِأَحْسَنَ مِنْهَا أَوْ

THE ONLY ONE

رُدُّوهَا ۚ إِنَّ اللَّهَ كَانَ عَلَىٰ كُلِّ شَيْءٍ حَسِيبًا

"When ye are greeted with a greeting, greet ye with a better than it or return it. Lo! Allah taketh count of all things."
-Pickthall

To say *yarhamuka-Llāh* [Allāh have mercy on you!] when anyone says *alhamduli–Llāh* [all praise is for Allāh] after sneezing.

عَنْ أَبِي هُرَيْرَةَ رَضِيَ اللَّهُ عَنْهُ عَنِ النَّبِيِّ صَلَّى اللَّهُ عَلَيْهِ وَسَلَّمَ قَالَ : إِذَا عَطَسَ أَحَدُكُمْ فَلْيَقُلْ : الْحَمْدُ لِلَّهِ ، وَلْيَقُلْ لَهُ أَخُوهُ أَوْ صَاحِبُهُ : يَرْحَمُكَ اللَّهُ ، فَإِذَا قَالَ لَهُ يَرْحَمُكَ اللَّهُ فَلْيَقُلْ : يَهْدِيكُمُ اللَّهُ وَيُصْلِحُ بَالَكُمْ. رَوَى الْبُخَارِي.

Narrated by Abu Huraira:

"The Prophet said, " If anyone of you sneezes, he should say 'Al-Hamduli l-lah' (Praise be to Allah), and his (Muslim) brother or companion should say to him, 'Yar-hamuka-l-lah' (May Allah bestow his Mercy on you). When the latter says 'Yar-hamuka-llah", the former should say, 'Yahdikumul-lah wa Yuslih balakum' (May Allah give you guidance and improve your condition)."

To NOT cause harm to anyone unjustly.

6:151 Quran

قُل تَعَالَوْا أَتْلُ مَا حَرَّمَ رَبُّكُمْ عَلَيْكُمْ أَلَّا تُشْرِكُواْ بِهِ شَيْئًا وَبِالْوَالِدَيْنِ إِحْسَانًا وَلَا تَقْتُلُواْ أَوْلَادَكُم مِّنْ إِمْلَاقٍ نَّحْنُ نَرْزُقُكُمْ وَإِيَّاهُمْ وَلَا تَقْرَبُواْ الْفَوَاحِشَ مَا ظَهَرَ مِنْهَا وَمَا بَطَنَ وَلَا تَقْتُلُواْ النَّفْسَ الَّتِي حَرَّمَ اللَّهُ إِلَّا بِالْحَقِّ ذَلِكُمْ وَصَّاكُم بِهِ لَعَلَّكُمْ تَعْقِلُونَ.

Say: Come, I will recite unto you that which your Lord hath made a sacred duty for you: That ye ascribe no thing as partner unto Him and that ye do good to parents, and that ye slay not your children because of penury - We provide for you and for them - and that ye draw not nigh to lewd things whether open or concealed. And that ye slay not the life which Allah hath made sacred, save in the course of justice. This He hath command you, in order that ye may discern." - Pickthall

To abstain from games and amusements contrary to the Shariah.

To remove pebbles, stones, thorns, sticks, and the like from the road.

$$وَأَدناها إِمَاطَةُ الأَذَى عَنِ الطَّريقِ$$

The lowest is the removal of harm from the road.

Dear reader, for a believer to have a complete faith in the oneness of God, they should have all these branches for the faith to be strong and accepted by God Almighty. All these branches are mentioned in the Quran and the sunnah of our beloved prophet Muhammad, peace and blessing of Allah be upon him. To understand them all, try to find their evidence, because I just gave you some as a teacher.

The Road to success

No one likes to be a loser in this world and hereafter and that is why people work so hard to achieve success everywhere they go.even the young ones have dreams to become doctors and teachers.

The question is, what is the connection between the oneness of God and the road to success? The answer is, without Tawhid or the oneness of God, there is no success, and that is why the prophet said:

عتبان بن مالك – رضي الله عنه – عن النبي – صلى الله عليه وسلم – أنه قال: « فَإِنَّ اللَّهَ قَدْ حَرَّمَ عَلَى النَّارِ مَنْ قَالَ لاَ إِلَهَ إِلاَّ اللَّهُ . يَبْتَغِى بِذَلِكَ وَجْهَ اللَّهِ » أخرجه الشيخان،

"Itban bin Malik may Allah be pleased with him said the prophet of Allah said Allah has forbidden the hellfire for anyone who says there is no God worthy of worship except Allah seeking only to please Allah. Related by Bukhari and

Muslim. "

The road to success is to be saved from hellfire and to get the glad tidings of going to paradise. That is why the prophet said that in saying there is no God worthy of worship except Allah you will be successful.

Allah talks about successful people in a chapter called Muminun, meaning believers, and the chapter starts this way:

$$\text{قَدْ أَفْلَحَ الْمُؤْمِنُونَ}$$

23:1 Quran

"Successful indeed are the believers" - Dr. Mustafa Khattab, the Clear Quran

The believers are successful because they took the road to success, which is to believe only one true God without associating anything with him.

عُمَرُ بْنُ الْخَطَّابِ، قَالَ لَمَّا كَانَ يَوْمُ خَيْبَرَ أَقْبَلَ نَفَرٌ مِنْ صَحَابَةِ النَّبِيِّ صلى الله عليه وسلم فَقَالُوا فُلَانٌ شَهِيدٌ فُلَانٌ شَهِيدٌ حَتَّى مَرُّوا عَلَى رَجُلٍ فَقَالُوا فُلَانٌ شَهِيدٌ فَقَالَ رَسُولُ اللَّهِ صلى الله عليه وسلم » كَلَّا إِنِّي رَأَيْتُهُ فِي النَّارِ فِي بُرْدَةٍ غَلَّهَا أَوْ

84

عَبَاءَةٍ » . ثُمَّ قَالَ رَسُولُ اللَّهِ صلى الله
عليه وسلم » يَا ابْنَ الْخَطَّابِ اذْهَبْ
فَنَادِ فِي النَّاسِ إِنَّهُ لَا يَدْخُلُ اَلْجَنَّةَ إِلاَّ
الْمُؤْمِنُونَ » . قَالَ فَخَرَجْتُ فَنَادَيْتُ » أَلَا
إِنَّهُ لاَ يَدْخُلُ الْجَنَّةَ إِلاَّ الْمُؤْمِنُونَ » .

"It is narrated on the authority of 'Umar b. Khattab that
when it was the day of Khaibar, a party of Companions of
the Apostle (may peace be upon him) came there and said: So
and so is a martyr, till they happened to pass by a man and
said: So and so is a martyr. Upon this the Messenger of Allah
remarked: Nay, not so verily I have seen him in the Fire for the
garment or cloak that he had stolen from the booty, Then the
Messenger of Allah (may peace be upon him) said: Umar son
of Khattab, go and announce to the people that none but the
believers shall enter Paradise. He ('Umar b. Khattab) narrated:
I went out and proclaimed: Verily none but the believers would
enter Paradise."

According to the hadith above, the successful people are
the people who testify there is one true God and worship him.
They will enter paradise because they succeed in everything.

Allah says if you enter paradise and you are saved from the
hellfire, you are successful, and that is the kind of success we
should work for.

Said Osman

3:185 Quran

فَمَن زُحْزِحَ عَنِ النَّارِ وَأُدْخِلَ الْجَنَّةَ فَقَدْ فَازَ

"Whoever has been kept away from the Fire and admitted to Paradise has really succeeded."

The road to success is to believe the oneness of God and to be steadfast without disobeying his orders that was the advice given to sufyan bin Abdullahi

عن سفيان بن عبد الله الثقفي، قال : قلتُ : يا رسولَ الله، قل لي في الإسلامِ قولًا لا أسألُ عنه أحدًا بعدَك . قال : « قُل : آمنتُ بالله، فاستقم »

Sufyan bin Abdullahi Athaqafi said, "I said, 'O messenger of Allah ,say for me in Islam a saying which I will not ask anyone after you.' The Prophet said, say I believe Allah, then be steadfast.'"

Allah is explaining to us that believing in his oneness is every success we are looking for. Let's ponder upon this verse in chapter nine of the holy Quran. This is what it says.

9:72 Quran

وَعَدَ اللَّهُ الْمُؤْمِنِينَ وَالْمُؤْمِنَاتِ جَنَّاتٍ تَجْرِي مِن تَحْتِهَا الْأَنْهَارُ خَالِدِينَ فِيهَا وَمَسَاكِنَ طَيِّبَةً فِي جَنَّاتِ عَدْنٍ وَرِضْوَانٌ مِّنَ اللَّهِ أَكْبَرُ ذَلِكَ هُوَ الْفَوْزُ الْعَظِيمُ.

"God has promised the believers, both men and women, Gardens graced with flowing streams where they will remain; good, peaceful homes in Gardens of lasting bliss; and- greatest of all- God's good pleasure. That is the supreme triumph." - Abdul Haleem

When we talk about success, it isn't about having a lot of wealth or becoming famous between the people to become successful is to attain place in heaven or paradise.

Let's see the Jewish boy who took the road to success and accepted the oneness of God. He declared the testimony during his death, when the Prophet presented to him while the father of the son was there.

عَنْ أَنَسٍ ـ رضى الله عنه ـ قَالَ كَانَ غُلَامٌ يَهُودِيٌّ يَخْدُمُ النَّبِيَّ صلى الله عليه وسلم فَمَرِضَ، فَأَتَاهُ النَّبِيُّ صلى الله عليه وسلم

87

يَعُودُهُ، فَقَعَدَ عِنْدَ رَأْسِه فَقَالَ لَهُ « أَسْلِمْ
». فَنَظَرَ إِلَى أَبِيهِ وَهْوَ عِنْدَهُ فَقَالَ لَهُ أَطِعْ
أَبَا الْقَاسِمِ صلى الله عليه وسلم. فَأَسْلَمَ،
فَخَرَجَ النَّبِيُّ صلى الله عليه وسلم وَهْوَ
يَقُولُ « الْحَمْدُ لِلَّهِ الَّذِي أَنْقَذَهُ مِنَ النَّارِ
.«

Anas narrates"

"A young Jewish boy used to serve the Prophet and he became sick. So the Prophet went to visit him. He sat near his head and asked him to embrace Islam. The boy looked at his father, who was sitting there; the latter told him to obey Abul Qasim and the boy embraced Islam. The Prophet came out saying: "Praises be to Allah Who saved the boy from the Hell-fire."

The road to success was given to this boy from above. That is why he accepted Islam and the oneness of God, which made the Prophet happy by saying, "Praises be to Allah Who saved the boy from the Hell-fire."

When the companions of the Prophet were preaching the oneness of God, they were going through hardship they were told to be patient, because that is a way to be successful when a hardship comes.

THE ONLY ONE

3:200 Quran

$$\text{يَا أَيُّهَا الَّذِينَ آمَنُوا اصْبِرُوا وَصَابِرُوا وَرَابِطُوا وَاتَّقُوا اللَّهَ لَعَلَّكُمْ تُفْلِحُونَ}$$

Sahih International: "O you who have believed, persevere and endure and remain stationed and fear Allah that you may be successful."

The family of Yasir went through this hardship we are talking about when they received punishment from Quraysh, until the mother and the dad of Yasir and Sumayah died through this punishment. They got the promise of entering paradise because they died for their belief in the oneness of Allah.

According to the Quran, success is based on where the people end up when the judgment happens on them.

59:20 Quran

$$\text{لا يَسْتَوِي أَصْحَابُ النَّارِ وَأَصْحَابُ الْجَنَّةِ أَصْحَابُ الْجَنَّةِ هُمُ الْفَائِزُونَ.}$$

"The residents of the Fire cannot be equal to the residents of Paradise. Only the residents of Paradise will be successful." - Dr. Mustafa Khattab, the Clear Quran

Success is also staying away from worshipping others than God, purifying oneself from any sins, and doing good actions."

91:9 Quran

قَدْ أَفْلَحَ مَنْ زَكَّاهَا

"Successful indeed is the one who purifies their soul,"- Dr. Mustafa Khattab, the Clear Quran

11:88 Quran

إِنْ أُرِيدُ إِلَّا الْإِصْلَاحَ مَا اسْتَطَعْتُ وَمَا
تَوْفِيقِي إِلَّا بِاللَّهِ عَلَيْهِ تَوَكَّلْتُ وَإِلَيْهِ أُنِيبُ

"I only intend reform to the best of my ability. My success comes only through Allah. In Him I trust and to Him I turn." - Dr. Mustafa Khattab, the Clear Quran

What are the things that if you do them you can be successful and become close to the creator?

Remembrance of God has success behind it, which makes life easy when the person remembers God.

THE ONLY ONE

20:124 Quran

وَمَنْ أَعْرَضَ عَنْ ذِكْرِي فَإِنَّ لَهُ مَعِيشَةً ضَنكاً وَنَحْشُرُهُ يَوْمَ الْقِيَامَةِ أَعْمَى

"And whoever turns away from My remembrance - indeed, he will have a depressed [i.e., difficult] life, and We will gather [i.e., raise] him on the Day of Resurrection blind." - Saheeh International

2:201 Quran

وَمِنْهُم مَّن يَقُولُ رَبَّنَا آتِنَا فِي الدُّنْيَا حَسَنَةً وَفِي الآخِرَةِ حَسَنَةً وَقِنَا عَذَابَ النَّارِ.

"But among them is he who says, "Our Lord, give us in this world [that which is] good and in the Hereafter [that which is] good and protect us from the punishment of the Fire."- Saheeh International

By reading the Quran's view about success, you will soon notice a change in your outlook about life. You will find it easy to be in a state of gratitude and happiness. You will find your worldly affairs being taken care of, and your heart will constantly yearn for Jannah and seek the means to attain Jannah. You will begin to wonder whether Allah is pleased with you or not for every act that you perform, whether they are deen or world related. When you have reached this beautiful state of faith, realize that this is the definition of true success in Islam.

To enter into the fold of Islam and to accept the concept of Tawhid is also the way to success, as we can see from this saying of the Prophet narrated by Abdullah bin 'Amr bin Al-'as

"Successful is the one who enters the fold of Islam and is provided with sustenance which is sufficient for his day's needs, and Allah makes him content with what He has bestowed upon him." [Muslim].

The one who believes the oneness of God will have a connection with God through prayer, which is a way of success. That is why when the caller to prayer is making Adhan, he says come to success.

حي على الفلاح

24:52 Quran

مَن يُطِعِ اللَّهَ وَرَسُولَهُ وَيَخْشَ اللَّهَ وَيَتَّقْهِ فَأُولَئِكَ هُمُ الْفَائِزُونَ

"And whoever obeys Allah and His Messenger and fears Allah and is conscious of Him – it is those who are the successful ones."

From the above verse, we see that the fulfillment of spiritual needs is a determinant of success and cannot be ignored. Hence, there is a need to provide a plan for how to achieve success according to the Qur'an.

The believers of the oneness of Allah will be successful by getting mercy from Allah and a great reward.

9:20-22 Quran

الَّذِينَ آمَنُواْ وَهَاجَرُواْ وَجَاهَدُواْ فِي سَبِيلِ اللَّهِ بِأَمْوَالِهِمْ وَأَنفُسِهِمْ أَعْظَمُ دَرَجَةً عِندَ اللَّهِ وَأُوْلَئِكَ هُمُ الْفَائِزُونَ

"The ones who have believed, emigrated, and striven in the cause of Allah with their wealth and their lives are greater in rank in the sight of Allah . And it is those who are the attainers [of success]."

يُبَشِّرُهُمْ رَبُّهُم بِرَحْمَةٍ مِّنْهُ وَرِضْوَانٍ وَجَنَّاتٍ لَّهُمْ فِيهَا نَعِيمٌ مُّقِيمٌ.

"Their Lord gives them good tidings of mercy from Him and approval and of gardens for them wherein is enduring pleasure."

Said Osman

خَالِدِينَ فِيهَا أَبَدًا إِنَّ اللَّهَ عِندَهُ أَجْرٌ عَظِيمٌ.

"They will be abiding therein forever. Indeed, Allah has with Him a great reward."

In the same chapter, Allah talks about the success of the Prophet and the believers who believed his oneness.

9:88 Quran

لَكِن الرَّسُولُ وَالَّذِينَ آمَنُواْ مَعَهُ جَاهَدُواْ بِأَمْوَالِهِمْ وَأَنفُسِهِمْ وَأُوْلَئِكَ لَهُمُ الْخَيْرَاتُ وَأُوْلَئِكَ هُمُ الْمُفْلِحُونَ.

"But the Messenger and those who believed with him fought with their wealth and their lives. Those will have [all that is] good, and it is those who are the successful."

"Doing good actions is another way to achieve success as we see in the holy Quran the chapter of the believers."

THE ONLY ONE

7:8 Quran

$$وَالْوَزْنُ يَوْمَئِذٍ الْحَقُّ ۚ فَمَن ثَقُلَتْ مَوَازِينُهُ فَأُولَٰئِكَ هُمُ الْمُفْلِحُونَ$$

"And the weighing [of deeds] that Day will be the truth. So those whose scales are heavy - it is they who will be the successful."

The believers of Tawhid are successful because they obey Allah and his messenger.

24:51 Quran

$$إِنَّمَا كَانَ قَوْلَ الْمُؤْمِنِينَ إِذَا دُعُوا إِلَى اللَّهِ وَرَسُولِهِ لِيَحْكُمَ بَيْنَهُمْ أَن يَقُولُوا سَمِعْنَا وَأَطَعْنَا ۚ وَأُولَٰئِكَ هُمُ الْمُفْلِحُونَ.$$

"The only statement of the [true] believers when they are called to Allah and His Messenger to judge between them is that they say, "We hear and we obey." And those are the successful."

All the verses we have seen all talk about the success of

believers related to the oneness of God.

Success means a lot of different things to different people, so when you want to define it, define it in the right way, which connects you to your creator and his oneness.

The Creator

The creator of the universe is one, and he deserves to be worshipped alone. He creates the way he wants because he doesn't need anyones help. That is why we need to understand the concept of Tawhid.

The non believers used to believe God is one, but they used to associate anything with him in worship which corrupts the pure monotheism.

29:63 Quran

وَلَئِن سَأَلْتَهُم مَّن نَّزَّلَ مِنَ السَّمَاءِ مَآءً فَأَحْيَا بِهِ الْأَرْضَ مِن بَعْدِ مَوْتِهَا لَيَقُولُنَّ اللَّهُ

"And if you ask them Who is it that sends down water from the clouds, then gives life to the earth with it after its death, they will certainly say, Allah."

Said Osman

When we talk about Allah as the creator, that means he is the only one who creates the way he likes alone should be called lord because other things can't harm nor benefit mankind, whether people worship them or not.

He creates mankind in the womb of their mom the way he wants, and he decides what they should be because he is the one worthy of worship and no one is like him.

3:6 Quran

هُوَ الَّذِي يُصَوِّرُكُمْ فِي الْأَرْحَامِ كَيْفَ يَشَاءُ لَا إِلَهَ إِلَّا هُوَ الْعَزِيزُ الْحَكِيمُ

"It is He who forms you in the wombs however He wills. There is no deity except Him, the Exalted in Might, the Wise."

Allah is one in everything, including lordship and his will, because he knows everything. No one knows the past the present and the future except him.

6:101 Quran

ذَلِكُمُ اللَّهُ رَبُّكُمْ لا إِلَهَ إِلَّا هُوَ خَالِقُ كُلِّ شَيْءٍ فَاعْبُدُوهُ وَهُوَ عَلَى كُلِّ شَيْءٍ وَكِيلٌ

98

"He is Originator of the heavens and the earth. How could He have a son when He does not have a companion and He created all things? And He is, of all things, Knowing."

"The creator is one in his names and attributes, and no one can call himself all-knowing or the most merciful.

7:180 Quran

وَلِلَّهِ الْأَسْمَاءُ الْحُسْنَى فَادْعُوهُ بِهَا وَذَرُواْ الَّذِينَ يُلْحِدُونَ فِي أَسْمَائِهِ سَيُجْزَوْنَ مَا كَانُواْ يَعْمَلُونَ.

"And to Allah belong the best names, so invoke Him by them. And leave [the company of] those who practice deviation concerning His names. They will be recompensed for what they have been doing."

When we say Allah is the one, which is what this book talking about, it means everything beside him should be put aside in worship or in seeking help.

1:5 Quran

إِيَّاكَ نَعْبُدُ وَإِيَّاكَ نَسْتَعِينُ.

"It is You we worship and You we ask for help."

Oneness of Allah means when we need something from him, we should go direct to him, because he is the solver of problems. that is the pure Tawhid which should be in the heart of every believer.

39:3 Quran

أَلَا لِلَّهِ الدِّينُ الْخَالِصُ ۚ وَالَّذِينَ اتَّخَذُوا مِن دُونِهِ أَوْلِيَاءَ مَا نَعْبُدُهُمْ إِلَّا لِيُقَرِّبُونَا إِلَى اللَّهِ زُلْفَىٰ إِنَّ اللَّهَ يَحْكُمُ بَيْنَهُمْ فِي مَا هُمْ فِيهِ يَخْتَلِفُونَ ۗ إِنَّ اللَّهَ لَا يَهْدِي مَنْ هُوَ كَاذِبٌ كَفَّارٌ

"Unquestionably, for Allah is the pure religion. And those who take protectors besides Him [say], "We only worship them that they may bring us nearer to Allah in position." Indeed, Allah will judge between them concerning that over which they differ. Indeed, Allah does not guide he who is a liar and [confirmed] disbeliever."

Allah is the one who creates everything and puts everything into their right position it is part of the belief in Tawhid, which we should acknowledge.

82:6-9 Quran

THE ONLY ONE

يَا أَيُّهَا الإنسَانُ مَا غَرَّكَ بِرَبِّكَ الْكَرِيمِ.

"O mankind, what has deceived you concerning your Lord, the Generous,"

الَّذِي خَلَقَكَ فَسَوَّاكَ فَعَدَلَكَ.

"Who created you, proportioned you, and balanced you?"

فِي أَيِّ صُورَةٍ مَّا شَاء رَكَّبَكَ.

"In whatever form He willed has He assembled you."

When we say Allah is the creator, what is the relationship between Allah being the creator and his oneness? That is a good question. To believe Allah is the creator is one part of the Tawhid, or his oneness, without believing that the Tawhid isn't pure and free from association, that is why people who claim to be God were promised a bad punishment like the example of Herod or Namrud in Islam.

Let's see what Allah says about pharaoh when he claimed to be God or the creator of everything like the river in Egypt and the kingdom.

Said Osman

79:24-25 Quran

فَقَالَ أَنَا رَبُّكُمُ الْأَعْلَى

"And said, 'I am your most exalted lord.'"

فَأَخَذَهُ اللَّهُ نَكَالَ الْآخِرَةِ وَالْأُولَىٰ

"So Allah seized him in exemplary punishment for the last and the first [transgression]."

When Pharaoh claimed to be the creator of everything, or one who deserves to be worshipped, he went against the Pure Tawhid. That is why Allah will punish him for his two sayings of "I'm your most exalted Lord" and "Pharaoh said, 'Counsellors, you have no other god that I know of except me.'"

For these two sayings, he will be punished on the judgment day because he claimed to be the creator of the universe when he didn't have the power to do so.

When the servant understands Tawhid, he will be obedient to his creator, and he will do everything which pleases him, without claiming to be a creator of rivers like pharaoh.

THE ONLY ONE

43:51 Quran

وَنَادَىٰ فِرْعَوْنُ فِي قَوْمِهِ قَالَ يَا قَوْمِ أَلَيْسَ لِي مُلْكُ مِصْرَ وَهَـٰذِهِ الْأَنْهَارُ تَجْرِي مِن تَحْتِي ۖ أَفَلَا تُبْصِرُونَ

"And Pharaoh called out among his people; he said, 'O my people, does not the kingdom of Egypt belong to me, and these rivers flowing beneath me; then do you not see?'"

When we talk about the golden days of faith in Islam, people went through a lot of punishment from the disbelievers just to deny the creator and to forsake the oneness of God.

The family of Sumayyah and Yasir went through this test until The father of ignorance [Abu Jahal] killed her, using a spear to her midsection. Her husband Yasir died after her, but they didn't forsake their creator and the noble words of "there is no God worthy of worship except Allah and Muhammad, peace be unto him, is his messenger."

The oneness of Allah [God] is written in the holy Quran in many places to teach mankind that their creator is one and the angels are witness to that.

3:18 Quran

شَهِدَ اللَّهُ أَنَّهُ لَا إِلَٰهَ إِلَّا هُوَ وَالْمَلَائِكَةُ

103

Said Osman

وَأُوْلُواْ الْعِلْمِ قَائِمًا بِالْقِسْطِ لاَ إِلَهَ إِلاَّ هُوَ الْعَزِيزُ الْحَكِيمُ

"Allah witnesses that there is no deity except Him, and [so do] the angels and those of knowledge - [that He is] maintaining [creation] in justice. There is no deity except Him, the Exalted in Might, the Wise."

THE FORGIVENESS

As Muslims, we believe there are many ways someone can get their sins forgiven by God .

When someone says there is no God worthy of worship except Allah, then his sins will be forgiven, even if they are like the foam of the ocean as said by the Prophet, peace and blessing be upon him.

When we put the forgiveness part aside, the Tawhid, if you recite it, has other benefits which are written in the saying below.

عَنْ أَبِي هُرَيْرَةَ، أَنَّ رَسُولَ اللَّهِ صلى الله عليه وسلم قَالَ » مَنْ قَالَ لاَ إِلَهَ إِلاَّ اللَّهُ وَحْدَهُ لاَ شَرِيكَ لَهُ لَهُ الْمُلْكُ وَلَهُ الْحَمْدُ وَهُوَ عَلَى كُلِّ شَيْءٍ قَدِيرٌ . فِي يَوْمٍ مِائَةَ مَرَّةٍ . كَانَتْ لَهُ عَدْلَ عَشْرِ رِقَابٍ وَكُتِبَتْ لَهُ مِائَةُ حَسَنَةٍ وَمُحِيَتْ عَنْهُ مِائَةُ سَيِّئَةٍ وَكَانَتْ لَهُ حِرْزًا مِنَ الشَّيْطَانِ يَوْمَهُ ذَلِكَ

Said Osman

حَتَّى يُمْسِيَ وَلَمْ يَأْتِ أَحَدٌ أَفْضَلَ مِمَّا جَاءَ
بِهِ إِلاَّ أَحَدٌ عَمِلَ أَكْثَرَ مِنْ ذَلِكَ . وَمَنْ قَالَ
سُبْحَانَ اللَّه وَبِحَمْدِهِ فِي يَوْمٍ مِائَةَ مَرَّةٍ
حُطَّتْ خَطَايَاهُ وَلَوْ كَانَتْ مِثْلَ زَبَدِ الْبَحْرِ
رواه مسلم . »

Abu Huraira reported Allah's Messenger as saying:

"He who uttered these words: 'There is no god but Allah,
the One, having no partner with Him. Sovereignty belongs to
Him and all the praise is due to Him, and He is Potent over
everything" one hundred times every day there is a reward
of emancipating ten slaves for him, and there are recorded
hundred virtues to his credit, and hundred vices are blotted
out from his scroll, and that is a safeguard for him against the
Satan on that day till evening and no one brings anything more
excellent than this, except one who has done more than this
(who utters these words more than one hundred times and
does more good acts) and he who utters:' Hallowed be Allah,
and all praise is due to Him,' one hundred times a day, his sins
are obliterated even if they are equal to the extent of the foam
of the ocean.

If you want a hundred virtues to be recorded for you and
a hundred sins to be taken away from your book, be close to
this unique message, which is that no God is worthy of worship
except Allah. The Saying of the Tawhid is protection for the
people against the devil. The only person who will get more
reward is the one who said more while he is alive in this world.

The one who believed the oneness of God but did sins
will be taken from hellfire through this unique message of the
oneness of God.

عَنْ أَبِي سَعِيدٍ الْخُدْرِيِّ، رضى الله عنه ـ عَنِ النَّبِيِّ صلى الله عليه وسلم قَالَ « يَدْخُلُ أَهْلُ الْجَنَّةِ الْجَنَّةَ، وَأَهْلُ النَّارِ النَّارَ، ثُمَّ يَقُولُ اللَّهُ تَعَالَى أَخْرِجُوا مَنْ كَانَ فِي قَلْبِهِ مِثْقَالُ حَبَّةٍ مِنْ خَرْدَلٍ مِنْ إِيمَانٍ. فَيُخْرَجُونَ مِنْهَا قَدِ اسْوَدُّوا فَيُلْقَوْنَ فِي نَهَرِ الْحَيَا ـ أَوِ الْحَيَاةِ، شَكَّ مَالِكٌ ـ فَيَنْبُتُونَ كَمَا تَنْبُتُ الْحِبَّةُ فِي جَانِبِ السَّيْلِ، أَلَمْ تَرَ أَنَّهَا تَخْرُجُ صَفْرَاءَ مُلْتَوِيَةً ». قَالَ وُهَيْبٌ حَدَّثَنَا عَمْرٌو « الْحَيَاةِ ». وَقَالَ « خَرْدَلٍ مِنْ خَيْرٍ ».

Narrated Abu Said Al-Khudri:

"The Prophet said, 'When the people of Paradise will enter Paradise and the people of Hell will go to Hell, Allah will order those who have had faith equal to the weight of a grain of mustard seed to be taken out from Hell. So they will be taken out but (by then) they will be blackened (charred). Then they will be put in the river of haya (rain) or Hayat (life) (the Narrator is in doubt as to which is the right term), and they will revive like a grain that grows near the bank of a flood channel. Don't you see that it comes out yellow and twisted.'"

No matter how small the faith of the people was after they
entered hellfire, Allah will take them from the hellfire through
their belief and they be like a grain that grows near the bank
of a flood channel, as it comes out yellow and twisted. For the
groups to be taken from hellfire, Allah will look their faith in
the oneness of God, and they will be forgiven, and Allah will
put them in paradise.

Forgiveness of Sins

It was narrated from Mu'adh bin Jabal that the Messenger of
Allah said: "There is no soul that died bearing witness to La
ilaha illallah, and that I am the Messenger of Allah, from the
heart with certainty, but Allah will forgive it." (Ibn Majah)

Freedom from Hell

Narrated `Utban bin Malik Al-Ansari: who was one of the
men of the tribe of Bani Salim: Allah's Messenger came to me
and said, "If anybody comes on the Day of Resurrection who
has said: La ilaha illal-lah, sincerely, with the intention to win
Allah's Pleasure, Allah will make the Hell-Fire forbidden for
him." (Bukhari).

Dear reader, this Tawhid should be said only to win the
pleasure of Allah and to get a place in paradise.
Ubada ibn al-Samit (may Allah be pleased with him) said:

"We were sitting with Allah's Messenger and he asked if there
was any stranger – the narrator said: i.e. People of the Book
– in the gathering. We said that there was none. He said: Shut
the door, raise up your hands and say: "There is no god but
Allah." We raised our hands and recited the shahada for some
time. He then exclaimed: "al hamdu lillah! O Allah, You have
sent me with this word and have ordered me to teach it and
have promised me Paradise for it, and You do not take back

Your promise. Be glad, for Allah has forgiven you!" (Musnad Ahmed)

The Prophet teaches his nation some supplication which contains the Tawhid words, which, if they can recite it, they will be forgiven. This unique message isn't only for saying, but also preaching to the rest of mankind.

There is no god except Allah Alone, with no partner, His is the power and His is the praise, and He is Able to do all things. A believer's sins will be forgiven, even if they are like the foam of the sea. (Muslim)

Dear reader, how many times do you recite this sentence of faith, "there is no God worthy of worship except Allah," everyday? That is a question you should ask yourself, because if you say less in everyday, you should increase it more, to get more reward and forgiveness from the creator.

The three aspects of Tawhid

When you read the books of creeds, you will see the three aspects of Tawhid which are as follows: Tawhid ruboobeyah, Tawhid Al asmaa wa sifaat, and Tawhid uloohiyah.

Tawhid ruboobeyah means the unity of lordships and the Al Asmaa wa sifaat means the attributes and names of Allah, which are ninety-nine names which anyone who memorize them will enter paradise. Tawhid uloohiyah or Tawhid ibaadah means the unity of worship.

These three aspects of Tawhid were mentioned in the Holy Quran many times, and the best example is the chapter called An-nas, meaning "the people."

Said Osman

سُورَةُ النَّاس

بِسْمِ اللَّهِ الرَّحْمَٰنِ الرَّحِيمِ

In the name of Allah, the Compassionate, the Merciful.

﴿١﴾ قُلْ أَعُوذُ بِرَبِّ النَّاسِ

1. Say, "I seek refuge in the Lord of humankind.

﴿٢﴾ مَلِكِ النَّاسِ

2. The King of humankind.

﴿٣﴾ إِلَٰهِ النَّاسِ

3. The God of humankind.

﴿٤﴾ مِنْ شَرِّ الْوَسْوَاسِ الْخَنَّاسِ

4. From the evil of the sneaky whisperer.

$$\{٥\} \; الَّذِي يُوَسْوِسُ فِي صُدُورِ النَّاسِ$$

5. Who whispers into the hearts of people.

$$\{٦\} \; مِنَ الْجِنَّةِ وَالنَّاسِ$$

6. From among the jinn and among humankind."

Allah is the lord of everything, which is Tawhid ruboobeyah, and he is the king, which is one of his names in the Tawhid of Al Asma wa sifaat.

Note that denying part or whole of any of the parts of any of these three is shirk, and this division is derived directly from the Qur'an itself.

$$الْحَمْدُ لِلّهِ رَبِّ الْعَالَمِينَ$$
$$الرَّحْمَنِ الرَّحِيمِ$$
$$مَالِكِ يَوْمِ الدِّي$$
$$إِيَّاكَ نَعْبُدُ وإِيَّاكَ نَسْتَعِينُ$$

"Praise be to Allah, the Lord of the worlds. The Most Gracious, The Most Merciful. King of the Day of Judgment. You alone we worship, and You alone we seek for help."

If you break these verses down, you will see a correspondance with the three aspects of Tawhid. Rabil 'Alameen (Lord of the Worlds): Allah's right to Lordship (Rububiyyah). Ar-Rahman,

Said Osman

Ar-Raheem, Maliki Yawmid-Deen (The Most Gracious, The Most Merciful, King of the Day of Deen): Allah's names and attributes (Asmaa wal Sifat)

When the Muslims talk about these three aspects of Tawhid, they don't mean God is three in one, or one in three, but Allah is Lord, and he has names and also attributes that are only for him and no one can claim them.

5:73 Qur'an

لَقَدْ كَفَرَ الَّذِينَ قَالُواْ إِنَّ اللَّهَ ثَالِثُ ثَلاَثَةٍ وَمَا مِنْ إِلَهٍ إِلاَّ إِلَهٌ وَاحِدٌ وَإِن لَّمْ يَنتَهُواْ عَمَّا يَقُولُونَ لَيَمَسَّنَّ الَّذِينَ كَفَرُواْ مِنْهُمْ عَذَابٌ أَلِيمٌ.

"They have certainly disbelieved who say, 'Allah is the third of three.' And there is no god except one God. And if they do not desist from what they are saying, there will surely afflict the disbelievers among them a painful punishment."

The non- believers of the old age accepted this Tawhid in general terms, although they differed with regard to some of its details. The evidence that they used to accept this is to be found in several verses of the Qur'an, such as the following:

THE ONLY ONE

29:61 Quran

وَلَئِن سَأَلْتَهُم مَّنْ خَلَقَ السَّمَاوَات وَالْأَرْض وَسَخَّرَ الشَّمْسَ وَالْقَمَرَ لَيَقُولُنَّ اللَّهُ فَأَنَّى يُؤْفَكُونَ.

If you asked them, "Who created the heavens and earth and subjected the sun and the moon?" they would surely say, " Allah ." Then how are they deluded?

Let's explain more about Tawhid uluuhiyah and what it means. Tawhid uluuhiyah means all the forms of worship in or out word or deed should be to Allah only and none other than him.

17:23 Quran

وَقَضَى رَبُّكَ أَلَّا تَعْبُدُواْ إِلَّا إِيَّاهُ

"And your Lord has decreed that you not worship except Him."

4:36 Quran

وَاعْبُدُواْ اللَّهَ وَلاَ تُشْرِكُواْ بِهِ شَيْئًا

"Worship Allah and associate nothing with Him."

Every action we do should be for Allah only, and we can see this Tawhid in the Quran like chapter Kawthar, meaning "the River."

108:2 Quran

فَصَلِّ لِرَبِّكَ وَانْحَرْ.

"So pray to your Lord and sacrifice [to Him alone."

The three aspects of Tawhid are written in many books talking about this same subject. As a reader, you just have to read more to understand the details if I didn't explain it in depth.

To conclude:

The author of the book, Said Osman, presented in this book the first pillar of Islam known as Tawhid, or the oneness of God. It is the means of salvation for every creation in the universe.   After reading the book, you will get a full picture of what Muslims believe about the oneness of God, because it is good to learn from the books of every religion when you want to understand their belief.

As humans, we aren't free from errors, so if you see any in the book, that is my own weakness and don't forget to share it with us so that we can fix it with the help of Allah. Read the book with the intention of spreading goodness among the people, because the saying of the Prophet was conveyed from me, even if it is one verse.

This message is a unique message for whole of mankind which consists of salvation, commands from God, and promises for the true believers. The word Tawhid is the key to open everything that you need in your daily life.

Without Tawhid, life will not be easy, and the abode in the hereafter, after the day of judgment, will not be appreciated, because the key isn't there for the person to open the gates of Heaven.

After reading the book, you will get to know Tawhid in depth with evidence, which is the purpose the book was written for. Every act in Islam should be done for the oneness of Allah and to please him alone, because without Tawhid, the action can't be accepted by God.

In order to accept the action, the belief of oneness should be there and following the way of the Prophet, who was the teacher of Tawhid for many years. Finally, anything that benefits you from the book, make supplication to God to be on my scale on the day of judgment, and may Allah grant us the true meaning of Tawhid with his help.

About the Author

Said Osman was born in Somalia state called Gedo. He went through different places for his Islamic knowledge. During his early childhood, he had a supporting family who helped him to join different madaris (Islamic School) for him to finish the Quran. Said is also a comparative religion student. At the moment, he is a teacher and Imam in his home city of Louisville, Kentucky.

,

Made in the USA
Columbia, SC
10 November 2021